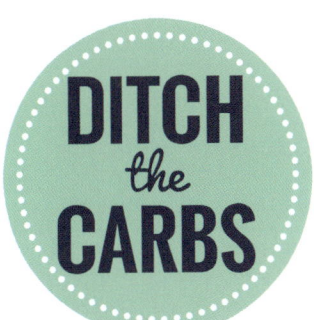

DITCH the CARBS

LOW-CARB LI

How to make real-food lunch boxes

40 easy recipes

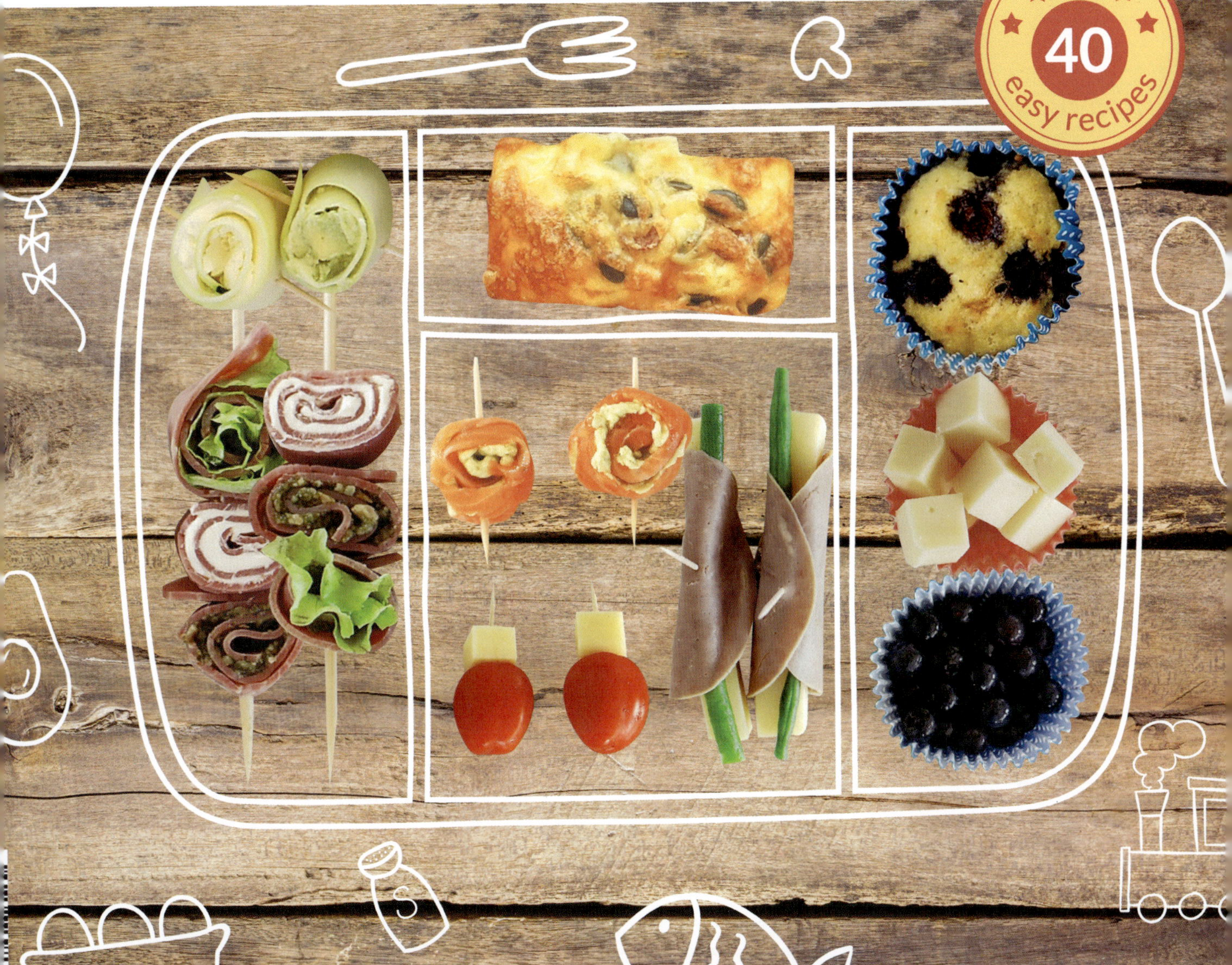

Sample menu | Shopping lists | Action plans

Libby Jenkinson

Copyright

Copyright © 2017 by Ditch The Carbs. All rights reserved.

You are welcome to print a copy of this document for your personal use. Other than that, no part of this publication may be reproduced, stored, or transmitted in any form or by any means, electronic, mechanical, photocopying, recording, scanning, or otherwise without the prior written permission of the author. Requests to the author and publisher for permission should be addressed via the website contact form.

USE OF eBOOK & WEBSITE

© 2017 Ditch The Carbs website is for personal use only. Please respect my work and do not copy or use content without permission. Anything appearing on Ditch The Carbs cannot be used for someone else's financial gain, otherwise you may be guilty of copyright infringement under the Creative Commons Attribution.

© 2017 Ditch The Carbs own the copyright to all images taken by Ditch The Carbs and copyright to all recipes created by me. I may give permission for others to share my work, but I remain the owner of all copyright images and words. All rights reserved.

You must obtain written permission before using any printed or digital media that belongs to Ditch The Carbs.

Nutritional values given in this eBook and website are as a guide only. They will vary considerably depending on which brand of ingredient you buy. For complete accuracy, calculate your own nutrition values using the brand of ingredient you have actually used.

Disclaimer

By purchasing this book you agree that anything included here or on the website does not constitute, or is a replacement for, medical advice. By purchasing and reading this eBook and website, you agree to be bound by the terms and conditions below.

Nothing contained in this eBook or the website can be taken as medical advice. Before undertaking a new lifestyle change, you must seek your own medical advice. My opinions are not intended as medical advice and should not be taken as medical advice and should not be a replacement for medical advice. Any lifestyle change may affect your health. Please ensure you are under appropriate medical care.

This eBook and website are for inspiration and practical guidance for this who choose to eat this way. This eBook and website are not intended as a substitute for medical advice or medical treatment.

Limitation of liability/disclaimer of warranty: While the publisher and author have used their best efforts in preparing this guide and workbook, they make no representations or warranties with respect to the accuracy or completeness of the contents of this document and specifically disclaim any implied warranties of merchantability or fitness for particular purpose. No warranty may be created or extended by sales representatives, promoters, or written sales materials.

LOW-CARB LUNCHES
How to make real-food lunch boxes

Libby Jenkinson

Welcome to

"Low-carb lunches How to make real-food lunch boxes"

I will help you make healthy, nutritious lunch boxes for your children, and you will learn how to remove junk food from their diet.

Welcome and congratulations! You are about to start making super-healthy, nutritious and filling lunch boxes.

We all dread the morning lunch-box routine, but "Low-carb lunches" will help guide you to reduce the sugar and junk food from your child's lunch box each day. It's not difficult, it's not complicated – it just takes some practical ideas to make it work.

This isn't about doing more; it's about doing things differently. I am a busy mum with three children and do not have time to make fussy recipes with hard-to-find ingredients.

I will show you how to cut back on the sugar and packaged food without spending hours in the kitchen each morning. I will show you how to cook *smarter*, what to cook and how to get your child involved.

Inside you will find:
- More than 40 easy lunch-box recipes, including nine exclusive recipes never to be published on the Ditch The Carbs website
- A five-step programme explaining how to give up sugar and carbs
- A 10-step action plan to transition to real food
- Easy swaps from junk food to real food
- A five-step plan for making easy low-carb lunch boxes
- Strategies for helping survive the change

Even making the decision to give up processed food and start eating real, whole food is a milestone in itself. The fact that you have committed to buying this book shows your dedication to the task ahead.

There will be stumbling blocks along the way, hurdles to face and tantrums (probably from you *and* your children), but don't worry. I will show you how to overcome these and not to dwell on them. Move on and be proud of any changes you have already made.

"Low-carb lunches" is perfect for those who just want to cut back on the junk, and for those who really need to knuckle down and go as low-carb as required to achieve stable blood sugars and weight control.

My family ethos is that we are low-carb, not no-carb. We focus on low-carb foods from nutrient-dense sources such as vegetables, nuts, seeds and low-sugar fruit.

All the photos in this book are my own children's lunch boxes. There are recipes, shopping lists, and even a sample meal plan for a week of low-carb lunch boxes. My recipes are all sugar-free, grain-free, gluten-free and low-carb. I use basic ingredients and nothing that is difficult to find. These recipes are perfect for beginners.

Let's get started.

Libby Jenkinson

Founder at ditchthecarbs.com

© Copyright Ditch The Carbs

Follow via

/ditchthecarbs

ditchthecarbs

ditchthecarbs

/+Ditchthecarbs

easylowcarbrecipes.tumblr.com

ditchthe_carbs

Ditch The Carbs

www.ditchthecarbs.com/subscribe-now

low-carb bread

Beef, chicken, pork & lamb 60

Meat-free dishes

CONTENTS

What is low-carb, real food? — 6
- What is low-carb, real food? — 6
- Why should children eat lower-carb? — 6
- 10 health benefits of living low-carb — 7
- Why real food? — 7
- What is real food? — 8
- Why sugar-free? — 8
- Why grain-free? — 9
- Why should carbs be lowered? — 10
- Why high healthy fats? — 11
- What is a healthy fat? — 11
- Why avoid low-fat products? — 12
- Fruit vs vegetables — 13

Tips to get started — 14
- Five-step programme: How to give up sugar and carbs — 14
- Easy low-carb swaps — 17
- Carb requirements for children — 19
- Low-carb and energy — 19
- Spend your carbs wisely — 19
- How much to eat? — 20
- Focus on real food — 21
- Why have school lunch boxes become so unhealthy? — 22
- How much sugar is in a regular lunch box? — 23
- How can you start to make lunch boxes healthy, fun and easy? — 24
- How to start: two simple strategies to help change into to a low-carb family — 24

Low-carb baking — 26
- Low-carb flours — 26
- Which sweeteners? — 27
- Properties of sweeteners — 28

Let's get started — 30
- Five-step plan for making easy, low-carb lunch boxes — 31
- How to be prepared for the week ahead — 32
- Emergency food — 33
- Packing lunch boxes — 33
- Packaging and lunch-box choices — 34
- Shopping lists — 36
- Lunch-box planning — 38

Recipes and ideas — 42
- Get organised: top tips — 42
- Simple ways to cut vegetables — 43
- Lunch-box fillers — 43

Just for the kids: Why? How? What? — 44

50

78

Snacks & sauces 86

sweet baking 90

Drinks 102

Recipes 48

Low-carb breads 50
- Basic bread loaf 51
- Waffles (sweet or savoury) 52
- Cheesy mini loaves 53
- Oopsies 54
- Focaccia 55
- One-minute muffins 56
- Basic bread rolls 57
- Three-seed bread 58

Beef, chicken, pork & lamb 60
- Meat wraps 61
- Bunless burgers 62
- Grain-free crumbed chicken 63
- Bacon-wrapped chicken 64
- Beef & bacon roll-ups 65
- Lettuce wraps (burritos) 66
- Sausage rolls 67
- Taco cups 68
- Meat-lovers' Fathead pizza 70
- Chicken "nuggets" 72
- Mini meatloaf 73
- Pinwheels 74
- Scotch eggs 75
- Bacon & egg pie 76

Meat-free dishes 78
- Egg wraps 79
- Courgette, feta & mint fritters 80
- Salmon quiche 81
- Boiled eggs & cheese soldiers 82
- Spinach & feta flan 83
- Smoked-salmon sushi 84
- Tuna fishcakes 85

Snacks & sauces 86
- Parmesan crisps 87
- Pork crackling 88
- Traffic lights 89

Sweet baking 90
- Chocolate zucchini cake 91
- Coconut-flour cupcakes – three ways 92
- Paleo seed bars 93
- Chocolate cookies 94
- Blueberry triangles 95
- Blueberry paleo pancakes 96
- Chelsea buns 97
- Carrot cupcakes 99
- Coconut flour chocolate-chip cookies 100

Drinks 102
- Peppermint green smoothie 103
- Flavoured waters 104

What is low-carb, real food?

No sugars — No grains — Only healthy fats

Why should **children eat lower-carb?**

All children will benefit from simply lowering their carb intake, especially from highly processed junk food.

Eating unprocessed, real, whole food lowers their carb intake almost by default. By removing processed food from their diet (or limiting it), their meals will become healthy and nutrient-dense. Their blood sugars will be stable, their mood will be stable and their concentration will be improved.

Food such as cakes, biscuits, crisps, chips, sweets, chocolate and fizzy drinks don't belong in anyone's diet on a regular basis. Sadly, they make more of an appearance in children's daily meals than adults. Processed carbs are easy to grab, easy to pack and portable for the drive to after-school activities.

There are no vitamins, minerals and micronutrients in starchy carbs that your kids can't get elsewhere to feed their growing bodies – and other sources are usually far better quality. Remember, processed, beige food is nutritionally empty, whereas real food (vegetables, meat, fish, butter, nuts, eggs and some fruit) is packed with what your kids' bodies really need to help them grow. In fact, studies have shown that chronic elevated blood glucose caused by high-carb diets can be far more dangerous for children's growth.

10 health benefits of living low-carb

Many wonderful and amazing health benefits occur when we go low-carb and sugar-free.

1. Nutrition is improved because we are eating nutrient-dense carbs such as vegetables, healthy fats, nuts, seeds and berries
2. The quality of protein sources is improved because we encourage unprocessed meats
3. Stable blood sugars and stable appetite
4. Reduced risk of many modern diseases through reducing inflammation
5. Improved insulin sensitivity
6. Improved mood with stable blood sugars. A sense of calm is achieved by many
7. Increased energy and concentration throughout the day
8. Reduced your risk of the "big four" – obesity, type-2 diabetes, heart disease and numerous cancers
9. Improved skin tone and clarity
10. Improved concentration, improved mental clarity, improved sustained energy throughout the day

Why real food?

Children need real food that supplies them with quality protein, healthy fats, and some nutrient-dense carbs.

The healthy fats keep children fuller for longer, gives your child essential fatty acids, and supplies the fat-soluble vitamins A, D, E and K.

The essential amino acids from high-quality protein are essential for growth.

And yes, children can enjoy carbohydrates – but nowhere near as much as people think they need. All the carbs and fibre they require can be found in vegetables, nuts, dairy and limited low-sugar fruit. Stuffing kids with starchy, stodgy, processed, sugary foods does their bodies no favours at all. Wheat and grains are now found in almost all processed food and somehow making a product with "wholegrain goodness" somehow appears to be some kind of magic health bullet. Among the many problems this diet of wheat imposes, is that the phytic acid in grains have been shown to hinder the absorption of iron, zinc and calcium, and wheat can reduce blood levels of vitamin D.

What is **real food?**

Real food...
- has as little human intervention or processing as possible.
- is food that your grandmother would recognise
- is fresh
- is as close as possible to nature
- consists of ingredients, not products
- is not fake food with colours, preservatives, chemicals and other nasties
- should not have a long list of hard-to-pronounce ingredients on the label

Remember: if you're in doubt, don't buy it.

Why **sugar-free?**

Sugar raises insulin, which is our fat-storing hormone. Insulin drives body fat and drives hunger. Insulin also drives inflammation.

Many modern illnesses (such as heart disease, cancer and dementia) are diseases of chronic inflammation. Chronic diseases don't happen overnight; they take decades to develop and to be eventually diagnosed.

We are not adapted to eat as much sugar as we do in our modern diet. Sugar is now found in 80% of processed food. By the time a child reaches eight years old, they have consumed as much sugar as an adult would have consumed in their entire life a century ago. Recent studies indicate that sugar may actually compromise learning and memory as well as the ability to cope with stress.

Five top reasons to give up sugar:
1. Sugar and processed junk food crowds out nutrition. Sugar is far more harmful than just being empty calories.
2. Sugar is damaging. The chronic high blood-sugar levels leads to chronic insulin levels. This eventually leads to insulin resistance and inflammation, which is the root cause of so many modern diseases.
3. Sugar drives obesity through increased appetite and increased fat storage.
4. Sugar causes tooth decay, which is the biggest reason for hospital admissions among children.
5. Sugar increases your risk for type-2 diabetes and heart disease.

Why grain-free?

I hate to be the one to break it to you, but grains aren't all they're cracked up to be. Grains have been used for centuries to fatten animals before slaughter. Grains are used to make foie gras (fatty liver pate). Geese are force-fed grains through a tube directly into their stomach. You don't see this function of grains advertised on the side of wholegrain products.

The grains that are found in almost all processed foods these days are completely different to the grains our ancestors were raised on. Grains have been modified to be shorter (and therefore easier to harvest), more disease-resistant and higher in starch. Grains are grown, sprayed and processed altogether in a different manner to ancient methods. Insecticides used on crops are affecting the health of our gut, our immunity, and our ever-increasing allergies.

Never in the history of mankind have grains appeared at every single meal and snack. Modern processing and modern farming methods has left grains so devoid of nutrition that cereals and breads have to be fortified.

Breakfast cereals are closer to desserts than a hearty breakfast. They are made with cheap grains, fortified, and have added flavours, preservatives and sugar. Their excessive sugar can easily exceed our daily sugar limit.

> *Ignore the marketing fluff and wonder on the front of food packaging. Read the back-of-the-box nutrition label instead*

Walk away from anything with a cartoon character on the box. You know it will be packed with sugar and grains, aimed at children and their sweet tooth. These are marketing tactics used to attract children to pester their parents to buy highly processed junk food, whether it be a sugary cereal or chicken nuggets.

Ignore all the health claims, fluff and wonder that is on the front of packaged, processed food. They may claim their product is organic, free-range, spray-free, no added sugar, only containing natural sugars, packed with 127 vitamins, high fibre... but in contrast, when you look at the back of the box and read the nutrition label, you will find added fibre, added vitamins, added flavours (natural or not), high sugar (natural or not) and a high-carb profile. It may be organic, but that doesn't undo the damage the high blood sugars and high insulin that will follow.

And finally, don't be persuaded by health ticks, star ratings or such like. Many "foods" are formulated to achieve a rating depending on the star-rating criteria. You know this type of system is ludicrous when a chocolate cereal/granola can be awarded five stars, yet an avocado is only awarded one.

Simply by cutting out sugar and grains, we eliminate most of the processed foods. By eating real, whole food and cooking from scratch, we become low-carb almost by default.

Why should carbs be lowered?

Carbohydrates are glucose molecules stuck together

Important to remember: we are **LOW-CARB**, not **NO-CARB**.

Many people don't realise that all carbohydrates eventually turn into glucose in the body – whether it is whole-grain bread, potatoes, whole-grain pasta, brown, wild or white rice, quinoa, organic coconut sugar, honey and even oats. They all do the same thing: spike blood sugars – some more than table sugar. And when blood sugar rises, so does the insulin demand.

When we, or our children, switch to lower-carb meals and ditch the processed junk food, we almost become low-carb by default. We may still eat carbs, but the reduced carbs come from nutrient-dense sources such as leafy greens, non-starchy vegetables, low-sugar fruits, nuts, seeds and dairy.

We are the most overfed yet undernourished generation in history. Processed carbs don't keep children full for long. While kids can often tolerate more carbohydrates than adults, feeding them high-carb food won't sustain them throughout the day – they'll experience sugar spikes and sugar crashes, which make them feel much hungrier than they would have done eating real food.

Two slices of wholewheat bread will raise your blood sugar higher and more quickly than six teaspoons of sugar

Why **high healthy fats?**

As we lower our carbs, we also increase our healthy fats.

There are three macronutrients we eat every day: carbohydrate, protein and fat. If we decrease the carbs, we must increase the quality protein and healthy fats in our diet. That's not to say it gives us an open invitation to eat fried, fatty food – it's about increasing our *healthy fats* and at the same time *reducing our carbs*. If we don't reduce our carbs but increase our fats, we are on a high-fat and high-carb diet, the SAD diet (Standard American Diet). This is the most damaging diet which causes obesity, type-2 diabetes and heart disease.

Healthy fats are essential for hormone production, healthy brain function, tissue development, appetite control and absorption of fat-soluble vitamins (A, D, E and K). Children especially need omega-3 fatty acids for eye and brain development. Choose olive oil, butter, coconut oil, oily fish, nuts, seeds, eggs and good-quality meat. Encourage your children to eat their vegetables by placing butter, grated/shredded cheese, salad dressings and healthy oils on the table. Avoid seed oils, which are inflammatory and incredibly processed.

Healthy fats keep us fuller for longer. Healthy fats makes food taste amazing – chefs have always known this.

What is a **healthy fat?**

Saturated fats and monounsaturated fats are incredibly stable and are less likely to become oxidised. Oils such as olive oil, coconut oil, macadamia oil and avocado oil are simple, pressed oils. Butter and lard are naturally occurring from animals. Healthy fats are those higher in omega-3 (anti-inflammatory) and lower in omega-6 (inflammatory). A naturally occurring healthy fat is as close to nature intended it and requires as little processing as possible.

Vegetable oils such as canola oil, rice bran oil, soybean oil, sunflower oil, corn oil and margarine are unstable, incredibly processed and easily oxidised. They are high in omega-6 which causes inflammation at the cellular level. Trans fats are the most inflammatory. Varieties of these unhealthy oils are found in almost all processed foods.

Omega-6 is an inflammatory polyunsaturated fatty acid (PUFA), whereas omega-3 is an anti-inflammatory PUFA. The ratio of omega-6 to omega-3 found in the diet of our

Fried halloumi slices

ancestors used to be roughly 1:1, but in the modern diet its ratio is closer to 15:1. This ratio, caused by a reduction of omega-3 from whole foods and an increase in the use of processed food and inflammatory seeds oils in the modern diet, promotes inflammation and disease. We cannot avoid omega-6 completely, but we can minimise it by increasing whole food and removing processed food and seed oils from our diet.

By switching back to good old-fashioned saturated fats that have very little processing, we improve health and reduce inflammation. And don't worry, more scientific evidence is emerging almost daily that saturated fat is not implicated in heart disease at all. In fact, it appears to be cardioprotective. It is a diet high in refined carbohydrates that is more detrimental to heart health. Inflammation is the real enemy, caused by a diet high in processed food, seed oils and carbohydrates.

Why avoid **low-fat products?**

Firstly, low-fat products are generally more processed as they have had the fat stripped from their natural state. Secondly, most low-fat products are pumped full of added sugar and chemicals to improve the taste and texture. Avoid buying low-fat products for both these reasons.

Start comparing nutrition labels at the supermarket for low-fat products vs the full-fat version. Lite yogurts, for example, can contain 25% carbs compared to natural unsweetened yoghurt which is 4% or even lower.

Learn to understand appetite vs hunger vs boredom

Fruit vs vegetables

Children should be encouraged to eat vegetables over fruit – they are packed with fibre, vitamins, minerals, trace elements, antioxidants and phytochemicals. But many parents complain their kids won't touch them, preferring fruit every time.

The problem is, fruit and vegetables should never be seen as equal: fruit is incredibly high in fructose and carbs, so it should be limited to only one or two pieces per day (and they should only eat whole fruits, never fruit juice or dried fruits). Choose lower-sugar fruit such as berries, half an apple, a few slices of pear, and cut back on high-sugar tropical fruits such as pineapple and melon. To encourage kids to eat more veggies instead, these are my top four tricks.

1 Add more healthy fats. I know so many children who will finally eat broccoli when it is covered with butter, salt and pepper. Begin by putting butter, shredded/grated cheese or a delicious creamy low-carb sauce on their plate and on the dining table. The pickiest of kids may have to have more sauce than vegetables at the beginning, but remember this will be a slow and gradual process. Each time, give them a little more vegetables with their sauce, butter or cheese.

2 Allow children to become hungry. I'm not talking about starving your beautiful children, but stop the snacking (more about that later).

3 Introduce dinner-time rules. Our number-one rule when we first began living low-carb was, "*You don't have to like it, but you do have to try it.*" At the beginning, my children were allowed to leave one vegetable on their plate each evening. What they didn't realise was that I gave them enough of the other vegetables that it didn't really matter which one they decided to leave. After a few months, we stopped having either of these rules because their food repertoire expanded so much. There isn't much they don't care for now.

4 Disguise them. I am generally not in favour of disguising foods, because in the long run you want children to understand and accept what they are eating, but I do believe there is a place for it. Why not disguise and hide vegetables in food they already enjoy? Begin by making them new foods and tell them it's something else. I began by making mashed cauliflower and told my children it was a new type of flavoured mashed potato. I also began to add various new things and we would play "guess the hidden ingredient" (similar to the game that cooking shows play). Eventually they tried new foods enough times to realise I wasn't feeding them anything disgusting and they were pleasantly surprised how many times they thought they hated a particular food, then it turned out they actually enjoyed it. You can also hide grated/shredded vegetables in meatloaf, homemade ketchup, soups, muffins and even cakes.

TIPS
To Get Started

Five-step programme:
How to give up sugar and carbs

1. Stop drinking sugar

Stop serving your children ALL sugar-sweetened beverages. No more juice, fruit smoothies, flavoured milks, energy drinks, sports drinks and soda. No matter what health claims the food manufacturer gives you, they are all liquid sugar.

Almost a third of children's daily sugar intake is from sugar-sweetened beverages. Stop serving them. This is the quickest and easiest way to becoming sugar-free.

If your children really are hooked on them, try my simple tip. Dilute juice with tap water, each time reducing the juice you add to the glass and increasing the water. Eventually the diluted juice will become tasteless. Swap soda for diet soda; make your own sugar-free flavoured milkshakes. These is a temporary solution because eventually you must stop serving all sugary drinks.

2. Stop eating sweets and confectionery

This includes sweets, ice cream, dried fruit and candy. They're are all sugar bombs. Not only that, they contain questionable ingredients and unhealthy fats that should be avoided. Ignore any claims that some candy or ice cream contains real fruit juice or is organic. It's all sugar, simple.

Stop giving them sugary treats, and instead occasionally buy dark chocolate with the highest percentage cocoa they can tolerate. The higher the cocoa percentage, generally the lower the carbs and sugar. Start at 70% cocoa, then increase as they begin to enjoy it. My children love 95% cocoa, but it did take some time.

Start to say no to all the well-meaning people that surround you, that feed your children sweets. How many times are your children offered lollipops from their hairdresser, the DIY store, sports teams, grandparents and fundraisers in the false belief they are showing love or being kind? No one should show their appreciation or motivation with sugar.

The more frequently parents are strong enough to say no to sugar from others, it sends the message that it sugar is no longer acceptable. Ask sports teams to stop after-match treats. Ask your school to start a no-sweet policy (both from children and teachers). Remind stores they should not be handing sugar to children.

3. Stop eating cookies, cakes and pastries

Baked and fried goods are a nutritional disaster because of the mix of high sugar, grains and, in particular, unhealthy fats such as vegetable oils and trans fats.

Start making your own low-carb and sugar-free treats occasionally. Long term, you need to cut back on these, but at the beginning, discover new low-carb baking and make it fun. Find a few simple recipes and teach them how to bake. Learning how to cook is one of the valuable life lessons we can pass to our children.

4. Cut back on bread, rice and pasta

Simply begin by reducing how much you serve each week. Aim for one or two bread-free lunches each week and one or two pasta/rice free meals. Rice, bread and pasta have little or no nutritional value and are generally a cheap way to bulk up meals. Instead, bulk up a meal with extra non-starchy vegetables.

Make simple swaps such as lettuce wraps instead of tortillas, cheese cubes instead of crackers, and zoodles instead of spaghetti. Start experimenting with cauliflower rice, and make your regular stir fry with extra vegetables and bok choy. Ditch the rice altogether.

If this seems too hard at first, start by cutting back, each time adding in more vegetables or more protein or more healthy fats to keep them full. There is no deprivation when living low-carb – only healthy, vibrant meals.

5. Stop all sugar and flour products

For this next step, you will need to get serious about all the sources of sugar and flour in your food. People may say it is restrictive and you are giving up entire food *groups*, but what you are giving up is food *products*. It is only because flour and sugar are found in so many products that it appears to be restrictive. Even just 10 years ago, many of these products weren't available. Supermarkets looked very different to how they do now.

Stop buying cereal and granola as each box is finished. Don't make a fuss: just don't buy them again as you introduce your own homemade grain-free granola. If this is a tough one, how about only buying one box a month until you are ready to never buy them again. Look at what else is in your pantry – muesli/granola bars? Ready-made sauces? Crackers? Cake mixes? Maple syrup? Pancake mixes? Slowly throw it all away, or commit to never buying them again.

Once your children start this path to living sugar-free and low-carb with healthy fats, their tastes will change, they will begin to experiment with flavours and they will slowly understand the importance of eating real, whole, unprocessed food.

It is a lifelong way of eating – for lifelong health benefits

Easy low-carb swaps

Bread rolls	→	Lettuce or egg wraps
Soda and juice	→	Flavoured water
Tropical fruit	→	Berries
Cereal/granola	→	Grain-free granola
Hash browns and sausages	→	Bacon, eggs, veggies
Cakes and biscuits	→	Low-carb baking
Sliced bread	→	Low-carb mini loaves
Wheat wraps	→	Meat wraps
Burgers and fries	→	Bunless burger with salad
Ice-cream	→	Low-carb cheesecakes
Processed meat	→	Real meat, off the bone
Pasta	→	Zoodles
Rice	→	Cauliflower rice
Frosting/icing	→	Chocolate ganache
Toast and jam	→	Low-carb waffles
Pizza	→	Fathead pizza
Fruit yoghurt	→	Natural yoghurt and berries
Chicken nuggets	→	Bacon-wrapped chicken
Sushi	→	Smoked-salmon "sushi"

Eat at the dining table. Make it a priority

If you always eat dinner in front of the TV or allow your child to be on an electronic device, it needs to stop. To begin, make sure you set two nights a week that you MUST sit at the dining table together. Slowly increase the number of days you do this each week and you will see a marked improvement. Studies have shown time and time again that children and families who eat at their dining table eat a varied diet, eat more vegetables and fewer fries, and drink less soda.

Children who watch TV or who are on an electronic device will only graze on their favourite part of the meal allowing the rest to go cold. They do not concentrate on their food, do not engage in conversation and may have a multitude of other issues when they are a teenager. Teenagers who eat with their family fewer than three times per week have been shown to have a higher rate of drinking, smoking and drug taking. *"While substance abuse can strike any family, regardless of ethnicity, affluence, age, or gender, the parental engagement fostered at the dinner table can be a simple, effective tool to help prevent it."*

Studies show that Americans eat out 40% of the time. Not only is that damaging to your wallet, eating out is generally higher in calories, unhealthy fats and sugary drinks, and portions are larger.

Family dinners are also a contributing factor to a child's wide range of vocabulary. Children having conversations with adults improves their talking, thinking and reasoning skills.

Eat low-carb, real, whole food and plenty of healthy fats — it's that simple!

Carb requirements **for children**

Everyone has a different tolerance to carbohydrates in their diet, and everyone has a different insulin sensitivity.

Children who are active and within a healthy weight range can tolerate more carbs and are more insulin sensitive than a middle-aged person, a sedentary person or an overweight person. Those with diabetes (type-1 and type-2) are intolerant to carbs, so restricting their carbs will improve blood-sugar control and reduce the risk of diabetic complications.

I personally don't count how many carbs my children eat. They are active, fit and within the healthy weight range. But for other children, such as those who are overweight or those who have diabetes (both type-1 and type-2) may need to monitor their carb intake quite closely.

I have added a nutrition panel for each recipe for those who need to count carbs and protein. If carb-counting is critical to you, always calculate your own values using the brand of ingredients you have used, as brands can vary drastically.

Low-carb **and energy**

All food gives us energy, but high-carb food gives a blood-sugar spike then a crash soon after. The energy is short-lived and can prompt sugar cravings. Picky eaters are particularly prone to this, as they often snack and graze on processed foods that are nutritionally lacking, such as flavoured yoghurts, crisps, muesli bars and crackers, and end up skipping proper, balanced meals made up of real, high-quality food. When you lower the carbs on your kids' plates, they avoid the high/low blood-sugar rollercoaster – and those energy slumps.

Spend your carbs **wisely**

It is worth repeating, but we are low-carb, not no-carb. Our carbohydrates come mainly from vegetables, dairy, nuts and low-sugar fruits. Spend your carbs wisely and choose the most nutrient-dense carbs you can find. Remember, 10g carbs from a piece of chocolate is not equivalent to 10g carbs from an avocado. The chocolate has no nutrients, it will raise blood sugars, raise insulin requirements and cause a crash later on. It will crowd out nutritious food. An avocado has 14 minerals and vitamins, phytonutrients, and keeps you fuller for longer.

How much **to eat?**
Low-carb – Moderate protein – Healthy fats

Carbs

There is no strict definition of low-carb, but even just *lowering* your carbs is beneficial. Many regard 50g-100g total carbs per day for an adult as a starting point. For children, the emphasis is on reducing their processed carbs and providing nutrient-dense carbs instead. For those who need to monitor their blood glucose closely, they may have their own carb limit set by them by their health practitioner. You may wish your child to eat more carbs when beginning the transition to lower-carb meals.

Protein

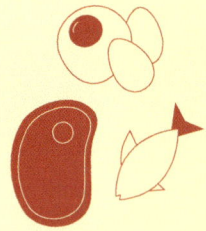

For adults, the aim is 0.6g per lb lean body weight (equivalent to 1-1.5g protein per kg). Too much protein may cause your blood sugar to rise, and too little can cause loss of muscle. Kids, however, are growing and need a lot of protein to meet all their growing requirements. When kids are hungry, generally they haven't eaten enough protein at the previous meal.

Fat

Eat enough healthy fats until you're full. Do not overindulge, do not eat to excess, but do not skimp on healthy fats. Your child should eat plenty of healthy fats to keep full until the next meal and to stop them from snacking. Only eat when hungry.

> **STOP EATING THE MOST OBVIOUS FOODS THAT CONTAIN SUGAR: SWEETS, ICE CREAM, CAKES, JAM AND BISCUITS. BY CUTTING OUT SUGAR, YOU IMMEDIATELY CUT OUT PROCESSED FOODS**

Focus on **real food**

A 10-step action plan to transition to real food

1. **START SLOWLY.** Be kind and gentle with your introduction of new foods. Depending on your starting point, and how poor your child's diet is currently, you may wish to only change one aspect per week.

2. **SLOWLY CHANGE YOUR PANTRY.** I never recommend doing an entire pantry clearout with children unless there is a medical reason that needs addressing immediately. Clear out the junk items you know you will never buy again, then when you eat up other foods, vow never to buy them again.

3. **PACKAGED FOODS MUST GO.** Each week try to stop buying processed, packaged foods. The first step is to remove the packaging from their current favourite snack foods and serve them in new containers or a new lunchbox. It will help them become accustomed to eating food with zero packaging. This will make the next transition to unprocessed food a little easier.

4. **GRADUALLY BECOME BREAD-FREE.** Begin by making one or two days' lunches bread-free each week. Increase until you are completely bread-free. I aimed for two days each week, then three, then finally we were entirely bread-free. Now, I haven't bought a loaf of bread in more than three years. It can be done.

5. **INVOLVE YOUR CHILD.** Allow your children to help choose recipes and ideas for their lunchbox. Give them some choices (but from a healthy list you have chosen).

6. **GIVE YOUR CHILD SOME CONTROL.** If your child is really struggling, let them choose one item each day that they are allowed to leave and not eat from their lunch box. Anything else that has not been eaten at lunch can be eaten for their afternoon snack when they come home – so they know you mean business.

7. **INTRODUCING NEW VEGETABLES.** Begin introducing new vegetables a little at a time, but the rule is they have to try it e.g: one cherry tomato, one cucumber slice, one raspberry. They will feel so proud they tried a tiny piece, and they may discover they do actually like it. This technique gets them used to trying new things with new tastes, and be more adventurous in their eating habits.

8. **TRY NEW SHAPES.** Cut vegetables into new shapes. A vegetable stick may be more appealing than a vegetable slice. Instead of serving carrot slices, give them cubes, grated/shredded, sticks, circles, hearts etc for variety.

9. **ADD IN HEALTHY FATS.** Start to add plenty of healthy fats to keep them fuller for longer. Make interesting dips packed with healthy fats. Vegetables can be the tool to eat the delicious dip.

10. **TAKE BABY STEPS.** Many, many baby steps will eventually add up to huge leaps. Make little changes; don't make them obvious to begin with, and choose one thing at a time to conquer. Make subtle swaps. It will be more sustainable in the long run.

DO NOT GIVE UP. It's not a race: one step at a time. Remember the tortoise and the hare story? Slow and steady wins the race.

Why have school lunch boxes become so unhealthy?

Life is busy. It's hard enough dreaming up dinner every night, let alone get excited for lunch boxes each morning. Well, all that is about to change.

Do you throw a slice of ham between some bread, grab a muesli/granola bar, a bag of crisps/chips, a fruit yoghurt and add a fruit juice? Or you might add rice crackers, organic fruit-juice strings, raisins and cupcakes. How about pasta and rice salad, sushi or doughnut? Pop them in the lunch box and you're done, right?

What may seem like innocent food choices, and maybe a treat, turns out to be a caring parent unknowingly carb-loading their kids all day long. To make matters worse, most children also began their day with cereal/granola, juice and some fruit. The poor kids are on a sugar roller coaster all day – no wonder they find it so hard to concentrate and have tantrums when they are hungry.

The very first step in making unprocessed lunch boxes and reducing the sugar, is to really *assess what goes into their lunch box already*. Even if it is full of "healthy" sushi, fat-free rice crackers, raisins, juice and a banana, when we analyse it, it is carbs, carbs, sugar, sugar, carbs.

The sushi is made of rice, sugar and sometimes flour. The low-fat rice crackers are highly processed and possibly fortified. Raisins, or any dried fruit, is no more than dried sugar. Juice has as much sugar as a fizzy drink. The banana wouldn't be so bad, if all the other products weren't in there too, but it's still high-carb (and therefore causes high blood sugars).

But don't worry, by the end of this book, you will see my five-step programme to begin your journey into low-carb, real-food lunch boxes; strategies to help the family transition to low-carb; easy recipes; and even a one-week meal planner with a shopping list for your new low-carb, healthy lunch boxes.

How much sugar is in a regular lunch box?

So let's look at an example of a regular lunch box in the picture below. You may be shocked when I break the items down into their carbohydrate and sugar values.

Orange juice (1 cup/250ml) = 25.8g carbs, 20.8g sugar

97% fat-free fruit yogurt = 14.7g carbs, 12.6g sugar

Raisins = 30.9g carbs, 28.6g sugar

Three sushi rolls = 20.6g carbs, 3.5g sugar

Banana (medium) = 27g carbs, 14.4g sugar

Organic muesli bar = 14.6g carbs, 8.9g sugar

Now, I'm not saying for one second that a child will have ALL of these in their lunch box, but many lunch boxes are far worse, with candy, chocolate, dried fruit leathers/ribbons and soda. This example of a lunch box will highlight how many carbs are in everyday lunch-box staples. There might also be pretzels, popcorn, home baking and crisps/chips.

On top of this, children generally start the day with some of the following: cereal/granola (62g); toast and chocolate spread (47g) or a smoothie (38g). Then there is the after-school snack, possibly another muesli/granola bar (15g), dinner or stir fry with a sticky sauce and rice (52g) followed by ice cream (47g) or an apple (25g) – you get the picture.

What I am trying to highlight is the importance of you to simply begin analysing what you and your children are eating now. And don't worry, it may seem impossible once you start doing this, but I will break down the steps you need to take into small tasks. You can begin by working on just ONE each week. You might need to go slower than this, or you may be on a roll and want to make change happen faster. It is completely up to YOU and YOUR family.

How can you **start to make lunch boxes healthy, fun and easy?**

Over the next few chapters, you will learn how to make lunch boxes easier. I will spark your imagination with new ideas and learn the tricks of the trade to cooking smarter, not harder.

Planning is the key to having healthy lunch-box ideas up your sleeve (or in your pantry) that you can pull out at 7am when life is turning to custard around you. Don't worry – nothing is tricky, nothing is difficult, and I am not going to ask you to cut cucumbers into a lotus flower to make it more appealing (who the heck has time for that carry-on?).

To make the transition to the low-carb way of life easier, you need to truly understand why going low-sugar and low-carb is so beneficial. You may wish to re-read the first few pages again. Because if you understand they *why*, you will be more inclined to stick with it when your little angels are whining and complaining (a parent's kryptonite). There is even a page at the end of this chapter written especially for your children, so they can understand, too.

How to start: **Two simple strategies to help change into to a low-carb family**

There are two methods to stop eating processed junk food, sugar and carbs.

1. Go cold turkey: clear out your pantry and start your new way of eating from today.
2. Start slowly: improve as you continue.

Which option you choose is completely up to you. You may wish to go cold turkey because having sugar and junk food in the house is too tempting. It can be quite cathartic and cleansing to throw away all your processed junk food and restock your pantry and fridge with real, healthy food. However, others prefer for it to be a gradual process.

Generally, I never recommend starting full throttle and having a pantry clearout when you have children to consider. Your household will be heard arguing from the next neighbourhood and you will throw this book right back at me. If it takes you a year to get lunch boxes sorted, then so be it. Imagine if you started a year ago – you'd be there already. The slower the better: build a routine, and make it sustainable.

The transition can be slow, easy, gradual and enjoyable. Considering your children may have been eating sweets, cakes, cereals, juices and bread for years, a few more weeks or months may make the journey an easier and more sustainable one. Personally, this is the route I used, and the one I prefer.

It takes a while for your tastebuds to adjust from the "bliss point" that food manufacturers have spent billions of dollars developing, to the wonderfully clean taste of real food.

Make little changes. Make baby steps. Work on just one element at a time and don't be discouraged.

Low-carb baking

Low-carb flours

It will take you some time to get used to baking with low-carb flours. You may be confused which to use, and how to use them.

Wheat flours
These are high-carb and contain gluten. Gluten is the protein in wheat that causes many people to have upset stomachs. Gluten also gives wheat-based dough and batter the ability to stretch and hold air in a pastry, cake or loaf of bread. Low-carb flours are naturally gluten-free, so do not have this characteristic.

Gluten-free flour mixes
Avoid these. Gluten-free flours are typically made from high-starch ingredients such as rice flour and tapioca starch. They are ultra-processed. Remember, *gluten-free junk is still junk*.

The two most common low-carb flours are almond flour (alternatively, you can use ground almonds/almond meal) and coconut flour. You cannot directly substitute these low-carb flours into your old favourite recipe. They work in completely different ways. My advice is to begin low-carb baking with recipes that have already been developed using these flours. Once you have become accustomed to the new low-carb flours, you will get a feel for them and know how much to use and how many eggs or how much liquid needs to be added.

Almond flour
This is the most popular low-carb flour. Almonds flour uses almonds that have been blanched to remove the skins then finely ground. Almond meal (or ground almonds) uses almonds including the skins. It is a little bit coarser than almond flour. Almond flour and almond meal can be used interchangeably in most recipes. Almond meal/ground almonds tend to be cheaper and you can make your own by placing whole natural almonds in the food processor and pulsing them with the blade until fine (but not for too long, otherwise you may end up making almond butter).

Coconut flour
This is the hardest low-carb flour to work with. I personally love it as it is much lower in carbs, much cheaper, and I am able to send my youngest child to school with coconut-flour baking. (He attends a school which has a nut-free policy, so almond flour baking is out of the question.)

Coconut flour behaves in a unique way. It swells and absorbs liquid many more times its own volume. So, typically, a coconut-flour recipe may require ½ cup coconut flour and use eight eggs. Many who are not used to coconut flour comment it has an eggy taste, but I flavour coconut flour recipes heavily. If it is a sweet recipe, I use plenty of vanilla; if it is a savoury recipe, I would typically use extra cheese, spices or salt. Coconut flour has a subtle coconut taste, so these extra flavours help disguise that.

Which sweeteners?

Our long-term goal is to give up the regular sweet baking, sweet treats and our sweet tooth. We want to stop relying so heavily on that sweet taste that can trigger sugar cravings.

You may want to recreate the regular sweet baking that your child has grown up with and loves. It can be helpful when you begin the transition to become a low-carb family to make low-carb baking a regular feature. This can help children feel like their lunch box is still a regular lunch box. This may continue for some time, but as the months go on, begin to reduce the baking and the sweet treats. It all goes back to my mantra of baby steps, slowly but steadily improving as time goes on.

When you first start low-carb baking, you may be confused with all the varieties of sweeteners available. Many brands give themselves the health halo of being "natural" or "unrefined", but what does that mean? My priority for sweeteners for my family is they must be natural AND not affect my or my children's blood sugars.

Many people argue they don't want to use an artificial sugar such as erythritol, and would rather use a natural product such as coconut sugar. They are confused between natural and processed. My rebuttal is always this: coconut sugar and erythritol are both natural and both processed, but erythritol does not raise blood sugars.

Even honey, maple syrup, dates and rice malt syrup are natural and processed but ALL will raise blood sugars. People also consume more thinking they have some small health benefit. The small micronutrients (the clue is in the term micro) does not undo the damage elevated blood sugars do.

Properties of sweeteners

There are numerous sweeteners available – more than I can comment on here – but these are the most common.

I don't rely on sweeteners regularly. They are for special occasions or when I want to do some low-carb baking. Long-term, we want to eat fewer sweeteners as we want to give up our sweet tooth and sweet cravings. Always add sweeteners in the minimal quantity, and adjust to your taste. As time goes on, your sweet tooth will diminish and you will require less.

	Natural	Processed	Raises blood sugar
Natural sweeteners that DO NOT raise blood glucose *			
Stevia	✓	✓	✗
Erythritol	✓	✓	✗
Xylitol	✓	✓	✗
Natural sweeteners that DO raise blood glucose			
Table sugar	✓	✓	✓
Coconut sugar	✓	✓	✓
Dried fruit	✓	✗	✓
"Refined sugar free"	✓	✗	✓
Honey	✓ ✗	✓ ✗	✓
Maple syrup	✓ ✗	✓ ✗	✓
Artificial sweeteners that I avoid			
Maltitol	✗	✓	✓
Aspartame	✗	✓	✗
Acesulfame K	✗	✓	✗
Saccharin	✗	✓	✗
Sorbitol	✗	✓	✗
Sucralose	✗	✓	✗

✓ ✗ Indicates the answers are dependant on the brand you buy. Please check labels carefully.

What I use and allow my children to have

- **Stevia**
  Stevia is 300 times sweeter than sugar. It can be bought in the supermarket as concentrated drops or powders. It can be easy to accidentally over-sweeten a recipe using stevia drops or powders. Stevia may give a slight bitter aftertaste if you use too much, which is why I like to use the blend of stevia and erythritol, which measures spoon for spoon in place of sugar.

- **Stevia with erythritol**
  Both are natural sweeteners but do not raise blood sugars*. Granulated and powder sweeteners are easier to use. They measure like sugar, behave like sugar and are unlikely to cause a bitter aftertaste.

- **Erythritol and xylitol**
  These are wonderful sweeteners, available as granules and powder. They have no bitter aftertaste and are easy to use in baking in place of sugar.

Granular sweeteners can be measured generally spoon for spoon instead of sugar. Check brands, however: some new ones to the market are double strength so only half a teaspoon is required to replace one teaspoon of sugar.

Caution with xylitol: this is lethal to dogs. Never feed your dog any low-carb baking made with xylitol, and keep it out of their reach. Similarly, chocolate is toxic to dogs, but is safe for humans to consume.

What I don't use

- **"Natural" alternatives**
  Sugar is sugar, no matter how natural and unprocessed it is. Honey, coconut sugar, molasses, agave, rice malt syrup, dried fruit and Medjool dates are all forms of sugar. Be suspicious when a recipe says "refined-sugar free" because it usually means they have just used another type of sugar and the author does not realise the implication these have on blood glucose.

- **Always check labels and brands**
  Always check the labels of ANY sweetener for all the ingredients. Many are blended with other ingredients which will raise your blood sugars. Dextrose and maltitol are well-known additives. They will both raise your blood sugars and should be avoided.

* If strict blood-sugar control is imperative to your health, please check how your chosen sweetener affects your blood-glucose readings. There are a small percentage of people who continue to have raised blood sugar from them.

Let's get started

- Five-step plan • How to prepare • Shopping lists
- Printables • Sample menu • Recipes and ideas

Low-carb lunch boxes are surprisingly easy – and fun. We have all grown up with the traditional sandwich, but is it really a good lunch? The wheat is 80% carbs, which means the kids will be hungry again within an hour, and wheat can cause leaky gut and malabsorption of vitamins. So forget the bread, which is just a bulky filler, and focus on what you'd usually put inside it.

Buy lunch boxes with little compartments and fill them with real food: quality protein, nutrient-dense carbs and healthy fats.

Last night's leftovers are the perfect way to get started. Use cold meat, such as roast beef, as a "wrap" and put a cheese and vegetables inside. I have so many ideas to share with you, so let's get started.

Five-step plan for making easy low-carb lunch boxes

1. **Protein**
Start by planning the main player in lunch boxes: protein. The rest will follow. Leftovers are the easiest way to get quality, deliciously flavoured protein into your children. If last night's dinner was spaghetti bolognese with zoodles, why not pack up a small container and pop it in the fridge? Add some shredded/grated cheese on top in the morning, and you're done. Or how about cold roast meat, cooked chicken drumsticks, quiche, cooked bacon, boiled eggs or a tin of tuna?

2. **Vegetables**
Cooked leftover vegetables are always easy to throw into a lunch box. Read my top tips below on how to have vegetables always prepared and sitting in your fridge. Try to vary how you cut fresh vegetables. Remember I said I'm not going to ask you to cut a cucumber into a lotus flower? But how about cucumber sticks instead of slices? Apple rings instead of quarters? Pepper/capsicum cups instead of slices?

3. **Sauces and dips**
Depending on which vegetables you have chosen, they will inspire you to add a sauce, dip or cheese that you know your child will like. In fact, sometimes the vegetables only get eaten BECAUSE of the dip it was served with. Try carrot sticks with pesto, cucumber slices and pate, or cooked broccoli with sour cream.

4. **Healthy fats**
Many of the protein and sauces will already come with their own healthy fats, but you need plenty in your children's lunch box to keep them fuller for longer, and more sustained throughout the day. Healthy fats don't usually come in isolation – they come packed with protein in the form of cheese, oily tuna, chicken with the skin and fat left on, and full-fat yoghurts. But if you want to add some extra healthy fats, why not add full-fat coconut cream to a yoghurt pot, olive oil to a salad, and homemade mayonnaise to an egg salad?

5. **Snacks**
Nuts, seeds, cheese sticks, pepperoni and low-sugar fruits and berries make the perfect snacks.

How to be prepared for the week ahead

- Plan five lunches each week.
- Create your shopping list and stick to it.
- When possible, do not go shopping with children. Their pester power and adoring eyes will always wear you down to buy something you instantly regret.
- If you need to take children with you, take them after a large meal so they won't be so hungry and so demanding.
- Peel and chop extra vegetables when making dinner each night. Place the vegetables straight into little lunch containers or ziplock bags so they are sitting in the fridge, ready to go. It takes only a minute to peel an extra carrot or two, but saves so much hassle in the morning rush.
- Cook a Sunday night roast dinner with extra vegetables, and do some low-carb baking. When dinner is finished, slice the meat and package the vegetables into little containers. You instantly have lunch ready for the first few days of the week, plus some low-carb baked goods.
- Don't go back for seconds – pop the leftovers in containers ready to go.
- Boil a few eggs each week and pop them in the fridge. They can be eaten plain or jazzed up into an egg salad, devilled eggs or added to leafy green salads.
- Love your freezer, perfect for all those double dinners and leftovers. Place the remaining in ziplock bags or small individual containers and freeze for another day. Paleo Scotch eggs (frozen whole), meatballs, quiche and meatloaf are all fabulous dinners to freeze.

Emergency food

Packaged goods to keep on hand or grab on your way home

When life is going crazy at 7am and you have forgotten to head out to the supermarket, you need a few pantry essentials. Or when you don't want to cook, but don't want to resort back to takeouts or packaged, processed food, these are some great options to have on hand or pick up on the way home from the supermarket or deli counter.

Long-life food for the pantry/freezer:
Tinned/canned tuna, seaweed slices, nuts, seeds, frozen berries, beef jerky, coconut chips, tinned/canned salmon.

Fresh food from the supermarket:
Mini cheeses, roast chicken from the deli, salami, pepperoni sticks, salad, boiled eggs.

Packing lunchboxes

Hot vs cold: the debate
There is always much discussion over whether you should send your children to school or daycare with a hot lunch box (and the problem of keeping it warm until lunch time) or a cold lunch box (and how do you keep it cold until lunch time?).

Food safety and the "danger zone"
The temperature at which foodborne bacteria is able to grow is referred to as the "danger zone". The danger zone is defined as 4-60C (39-140F). It is recommended that the time food is kept outside these temperatures should be minimised, and any food that falls within these temperatures for more than two hours is not consumed.

Cold lunch boxes
You will need to decide if you require a cool pack or ice pack to be included in your child's lunch box, and how long the lunch will be out of the fridge before eaten by your child. You may wish to buy an insulated bag for the lunch box.

Personally, I rarely send my children to school with an ice pack, and they always eat their lunches at room temperature. I also grew up eating my school lunch box at room temperature. The downside of ice packs is the condensation they produce inside the

lunchbox, or even onto the food. If you choose not to use an ice pack, food must be as cold as possible before adding to the lunch box. An easy alternative to a ice pack is to pack some food that is already frozen, such as frozen berries in a pot or a frozen smoothie in a squeeze tube. They help keep the lunch box cool and, by the lunch break, they are defrosted and the perfect temperature to eat.

Hot lunch boxes

If you would like your children to eat something warm at lunch, the food will need to be reheated safely in the morning, and packed in an insulated container so it remains warm until it's time to be eaten. You could buy a flask for liquids or a wide-mouthed flask for hot food. When buying a flask, check it is guaranteed to be leakproof, and that your child can open it by themselves.

Ultimately, the choice is yours: safety vs risk vs convenience.

Packaging and lunch-box choices

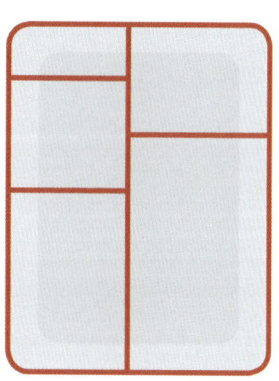

Bento boxes

These are undoubtedly the easiest of lunch boxes to pack – their little compartments make it a breeze to pop everything in for a quick and easy lunch. They can be made of plastic or metal, and some good brands are super sturdy and can even survive the dishwasher. The downsides? They can be very expensive and some are not leakproof; not all your food items can fit into the tiny spaces; and they can be fiddly to clean in all the corners. They are more appropriate for younger children than teenagers.

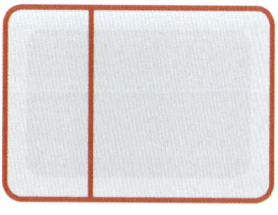

Regular lunch boxes

These are generally the cheapest to buy and easiest to clean, but require wrapping of all the food items individually. Some designs have the best of both worlds – they don't have all the tiny fiddly compartments of a bento box, but have two or three simple dividers.

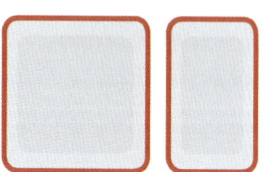

Individual containers

Plastic or metal small containers are great for putting almost anything inside them: leftovers, chopped vegetables, dips, sauces, berries etc. Make sure they are leakproof and sturdy. Cheap ones bend out of shape when washed in hot water and begin to leak. Little containers make life a breeze when you have very small leftovers. No matter whether you have one piece of broccoli, two pieces of carrot and one small tomato, throw them all in a little container and suddenly it looks like a vegetable medley.

Plastic wrap/cling film

Perfect for wrapping almost anything – just ensure that the one you buy is BPA free. My top tip is to make a little twist in the final piece of plastic wrap, so children can find the end easily to unwrap their food. I hear of so many little ones who come home with an uneaten lunch because they couldn't get find the end of the plastic wrap.

Ice/cool packs

These will help keep food in lunch boxes cooler for longer, but may also cause condensation. An insulated bag for your lunch box helps to prevent this. Even adding a pot of frozen berries in a leakproof container, frozen smoothie or a frozen yoghurt (unsweetened) will also do the trick. By lunch, it has done it's job of keeping the food cooled and is defrosted ready to be eaten.

Flask

There are ones for liquids and ones for food with a wide lid so your children can eat directly from the insulated pot. Make sure it is leakproof, insulated so the outside remains cool, and sturdy enough to survive the occasional drop on the floor from the school bag.

Never ever throw away leftovers –
they are the start of tomorrow's lunch

Low-carb lunches: How to make real-food lunch boxes | 35

Shopping lists

Stocking your kitchen for low-carb lunch boxes

At the beginning, check all nutrition panels for unexpected added sugar, hidden ingredients and other nasties. Once you get to know the brands you like and are safe to buy, you will shop instinctively and it will become quicker and easier.

Vegetables & fruit

- Apples
- Asparagus
- Aubergine
- Avocados
- Berries
- Broccoli
- Brussels sprouts
- Cabbage
- Cauliflower
- Celery
- Courgettes
- Cucumber
- Eggplant
- Fennel
- Garlic
- Herbs
- Kale
- Lemons
- Lettuce
- Limes
- Mushrooms
- Onions
- Pears
- Peppers
- Salad ingredients
- Silver beet
- Spinach
- Spring onions
- Swiss chard
- Tomatoes
- Zucchini

Meat & fish

- Bacon – off the bone (unsweetened)
- Beef – all cuts, mince/ground, steaks
- Chicken – all cuts, skin on, mince/ground, whole
- Crab – check it is not "crab-flavoured" meat
- Duck – all cuts, skin on, whole
- Fish – fresh or frozen
- Ham – off the bone (unsweetened)
- Lamb – all cuts, chops, roast, mince/ground, steaks
- Organ meats – liver, kidney etc
- Pepperoni – as unprocessed as possible
- Pork
- Prawns
- Prosciutto
- Salami – as unprocessed as possible
- Salmon – fresh, or canned in olive oil or brine
- Sardines in oil
- Sausages – more than 85% meat and with minimal processing
- Shellfish – mussels, oysters etc
- Shrimps
- Tuna – fresh or canned in olive oil or brine
- Turkey – all cuts

Fridge

- Bagged salad
- Boiled eggs
- Butter
- Cheese, full-fat – all types, e.g: brie, camembert, feta, mozzarella, Parmesan
- Cheese – packs of sticks/slices
- Cream, full-fat – heavy, double, whipping
- Cream cheese – full-fat
- Deli meat – pepperoni sticks, ham off the bone, whole cooked chicken, etc
- Eggs
- Milk – full-fat
- Sour cream
- Yoghurt – full-fat, unsweetened

Pantry

- Almond meal/flour/ground
- Canned/tinned tuna
- Cocoa, unsweetened
- Coconut butter
- Coconut cream (>20% fat)
- Coconut milk (<20% fat)
- Coconut flour
- Coconut, unsweetened – shredded, desiccated, threads, chips, fresh
- Chocolate (>80% cocoa)
- Gelatin
- Gherkins
- Herbs and spices
- Mayonnaise
- Mustard powder
- Nuts – almonds, brazil, hazelnuts, macadamia, pecans, walnuts
- Nut butters
- Olives – green, black, stuffed
- Pesto dip
- Pickles
- Psyllium husk
- Salsa, unsweetened
- Seeds – flaxseeds, linseeds, pumpkin, sunflower
- Sweetener of choice – stevia or erythritol
- Tahini
- Vanilla

Freezer

- Berries
- Fish
- Leftovers!
- Prawns
- Spinach

Healthy fat

- Avocado oil
- Butter
- Coconut oil
- Ghee
- Lard
- Macadamia oil
- Olive oil – extra virgin

Packaged and convenience food

- Beef jerky
- Canned/tinned tuna
- Coconut chips/slices
- Nuts – snack bags
- Pepperoni sticks
- Pork crackling
- Seaweed slices

Lunch-box equipment

- Aluminium foil
- Bento lunchbox
- Cupcake cases
- Flask
- Ice-blocks or cold packs
- Plastic wrap (BPA-free)
- Small containers of various sizes
- Water bottle
- Wax paper
- Ziplock bags

Kitchen gadgets and equipment

- Food processor
- Spiralizer
- Slow cooker
- Stick blender/immersion blender
- Waffle maker

Lunch-box planning

Fill this section with the help of your children. If you know what they like, it makes planning their lunch box so much easier. As they discover new recipes and foods, they can add them to their list.

Why not reward them each time they add two more items? Buy them a new book, take them to the library, play a game, go for a walk or a swim. Just don't reward them with food. It is how so many of us as adults have become emotional eaters because we learned at an early age to celebrate or commiserate with food.

Favourite-foods list

Protein foods	Vegetables	Sauces and dips

Low-sugar fruits	Dairy	Snacks

Lunch-box planner

	MONDAY	TUESDAY	WEDNESDAY	THURSDAY	FRIDAY
Protein foods					
Vegetables					
Sauces and dips					
Low-sugar fruits					
Dairy					
Snacks					

Sample lunch-box plan

This is an example of what you may wish to pack in your child's lunch box each day. You will need to vary how many items and how much you serve, depending on your child's age and hunger. My three children eat very similar quantities even though they are 10 (incredibly active), 13 (moderately active) and 16 (in the middle of exams).

If your child is just starting out, allow them to plan the week's lunch-box ideas, then you can use it as the basis to organise the week's evening-meal plan. Alternatively, simply plan your week's family meals, and make enough for leftovers for the following day.

	MONDAY	TUESDAY	WEDNESDAY	THURSDAY	FRIDAY
Protein foods	• Meat wraps • Smoked-salmon "sushi"	• Tinned/canned tuna • Bacon and egg pie	• Chicken nuggets • Pinwheels	• Lettuce wraps • Salmon quiche	• Mini meatloaf • Grain-free KFC
Vegetables	• Avocado • Carrots	• Leftovers • Capsicum/peppers	• Avocado • Broccoli	• Leftovers • Gherkins	• Courgette fritters • Baby tomatoes
Sauces and dips	Cream cheese	"Slime"	Red dip	Orange dip	"Slime"
Low-sugar fruits	Apple slices	Berries	Berries	Apple slices	Berries
Dairy	Yoghurt	Cheese	Yoghurt	Cheese	Yoghurt
Snacks	Blueberry triangles	Coconut chips	Seed bars	Lemon cupcakes	Mini loaves

Recipes and ideas

Get organised: top tips

- Each Sunday night, try to cook a meal such as a roast dinner in the oven. While the dinner is cooking, prepare and cook grain-free granola and some fun baking for the week ahead.
- Whenever you prepare vegetables, prepare extra and place them immediately in little containers in the fridge. They generally stay fresh for three days.
- Ask your children to help you bake and work out quantities. My children are superb mathematicians because I always asked them to adapt a recipe for me. Why not make 1½ the usual recipe? Allow them to work out the quantities required (just ensure they are correct before adding them).
- Never throw away leftovers, even if it is one Brussels sprout or one carrot stick. They can all be put into a container and called a "vegetable medley".

These are just a selection of ideas I fill my children's lunch boxes with.

Simple ways to cut vegetables

Don't worry, I'm not asking you to get out your cookie cutters or decorating tools, I just want to show you how to vary the shapes of your vegetables for the little children who really need some variation and to make their lunchbox fun. Squares, fingers, sticks, grated/shredded – just jazz up old, tired vegetable options, and your children may surprise you and eat them.

Lunch-box fillers

Because you will start planning your lunch box predominantly using leftovers, you will need a selection of lunch-box fillers. This may be vegetables, low-carb baking, healthy fats, extra protein and low-sugar fruits.

What is sugar?
Sugar is the sweet taste we get from ice cream, chocolate, cakes, biscuits, soda, fruit, milk and honey.

Why is sugar so bad for me?
Sugar has no nutritional value – no protein, no vitamins, no minerals, no fibre and no goodness. What makes it worse is that it makes you want more and more. Once you start a candy bar or a bowl of ice cream, it is hard to stop. Sugar causes tooth decay and bad skin. Sugar can affect how you behave, how you concentrate and how you think.

What is a carbohydrate?
All carbohydrates are sugars stuck together. They eventually turn into sugar inside your body.

Why are sugars and carbohydrates so bad?
When you eat or drink sugar or carbs, your blood sugar will rise, sometimes to dangerous levels. Then when the body clears it away, your blood sugar can become too low, making you irritable, angry, moody and hungry again. This up down, up down is sometimes known as the sugar rollercoaster.

Why does my family want me to eat more vegetables?
Vegetables are full of nutrition packed with amazing colours, fibre, minerals and vitamins that you cannot get from junk food. Your body needs all these amazing vitamins, minerals and fibre to help your body function and grow like it it needs to do.

Why should I cut back on fruit?
Fruit is yummy, huh? But it's also sweet – really sweet – and most kids eat way too much. Fruit is full of fructose which is a special type of sugar that the body has a tough time dealing with. It causes the most dangerous type of fat – belly fat. That dangerous belly fat around the tummy is wrapping all the organs with fat so they don't function properly anymore.

Why can't I have fruit juice anymore? It's healthy, right?
Fruit juice has all the sugar from a whole heap of fruit, but with all the fibre removed. A glass of orange juice isn't the same as the goodness from six oranges – it's the same as the sugar from six oranges. And many fruit juices aren't even made with real fruit. They are fruit-flavoured drinks, or just have a small amount of real fruit then have sugar added to them. Some fruit juice has even more sugar than a soda. And we all know soda is pretty nasty stuff. And when you drink fruit juice, all the sugar enters your body so quickly because there isn't any fibre any more to slow down the sugar being absorbed.

What's so bad about French fries? They are a potato, and therefore a vegetable…

French fries are more than just a potato. They are deep fried in unhealthy oils which cause swelling and inflammation inside your body. You can't see it, but this unhealthy oil is doing damage to you. Many fast-food French fries have more than a dozen ingredients hidden in them, one of which is sugar. And finally, most kids drown their French fries in ketchup – yes, more sugar.

What is this insulin thing I keep hearing about?

When your blood sugars rise, your body needs insulin to lower the sugar to a normal level. For most people, insulin is produced in your pancreas. For others, who have type-1 diabetes, they need to inject insulin.

What is the difference between type-1 and type-2 diabetes?

Even though they sound similar, they are completely different. Type-1 diabetes is a condition that some people are born with or develop at an early age. Their body can't produce insulin anymore, so they have to inject it. Type-2 diabetes can occur when a person has produced so much insulin through years and years of eating a high-carb diet that their poor pancreas can't cope any more. They eventually may have to start medication or injections. Type-2 diabetes used to be called sugar diabetes.

Why do I get ratty after eating too much sugar?

If you eat a lot of sugar, your insulin works overtime to remove all the excess sugar from your bloodstream so it enters your cells. This rush of sugar gives you a burst of energy which is then followed by a huge drop in sugar levels from all the insulin released. The drop in sugar makes you ratty, grumpy, irritable and may cause you to find it hard to concentrate at school.

What short-term health effects will sugar cause?

Sugar can lower your immune system and so you might get coughs and colds easily. Sugar can also affect all the good bacteria in your tummy, which helps you feel happy and sleep well. Sugar can cause pimples and bad skin. Sugar causes bad breath and tooth decay.

What long-term health effects does it have?

If you eat too much junk food, such as French fries, chicken nuggets and soda, you will not get all the vitamins and building blocks your growing body needs. Imagine if you were building a toy but you had a missing part. It doesn't work, does it? And it's tough to add the missing part later if you have already made it. Well, it's like that in your body. If you are missing an essential vitamin, protein, mineral as you are growing, there may be some areas which don't develop quite right.

Too much junk, too much sugar and not enough healthy foods have been linked with many disease that older people have such as heart disease, obesity, dementia, high blood pressure, cancer, and depression. It can also cause problems that children suffer from, such as allergies, ADHD and asthma.

How much sugar is OK?
The American Heart Association recommends no more than three teaspoons of sugar per day for children, but some kids are having up to 23 teaspoons per day! Pretty alarming, huh? Most kids overdo their sugar limit each morning by eating just one bowl of cereal/granola.

Where is sugar hiding?
Some food which you think is healthy actually isn't. There is sugar hiding in cereal/granola bars, fruit yoghurts, ketchup and even tinned/canned tuna!

Are low-fat products better for me?
No, sorry. When food manufacturers take the natural fat from a food, it is left tasting pretty gross. So what do they do? They pump in sugar and chemicals to make it taste nice again. So go for the naturally full-fat products that haven't been messed about with in a factory.

Will sugar rot my teeth?
I'm afraid so. Sugar definitely cause tooth decay and cavities. The soda washes your teeth in sugar as you drink it. The sugar and acid attacks the surface (enamel) of your lovely bright teeth and eventually causes them to start rotting away. And as for those chewy sweets? They are even worse because they end up sticking on your teeth for hours and hours.

What am I allowed to eat after I cut back on sugar?
There are so many amazing sugar-free recipes. Do you love cheesecake? Pizza? Spaghetti? Sausage rolls? Stuffed chicken? Well, they can be made into healthier versions without added sugar, and with real food that hasn't been messed about with in a factory somewhere. Eat food your great-great grandmother would recognise. Eat fresh food. Ask if you can start cooking some new sugar-free recipes. Have fun in the kitchen and start experimenting making your own recipes. Go for it and have fun.

RECIPES

- Low-carb bread
- Beef, chicken & lamb
- Meat-free dishes
- Snacks & sauces
- Sweet baking
- Drinks

LOW-CARB BREAD

Basic bread loaf | Waffles (sweet or savoury) | Cheesy mini loaves | Oopsies | Focaccia | One-minute muffins | Basic bread rolls | Three-seed bread

Basic bread loaf

Makes	Serving
1 loaf (15 slices)	1 slice

Nutrition per serving: Calories: 116 | Total fat: 9.9g | Total carbs: 3.5g | Fibre: 1.6g | Sugars: 0.9g | Protein: 4.3g

A basic low-carb bread loaf is the perfect substitute for a traditional sliced loaf. It is an adaptable recipe, so play around with adding flavours, herbs, spices and cheese. Let your children help with baking and they can add what they prefer. Pizza bread, anyone?

- 200g/7oz full-fat cream cheese
- 100g/1 cup almond meal/flour
- 2 tbsp coconut flour
- 2 tbsp psyllium husk
- ½ tsp salt
- 1 tsp baking powder
- 5 eggs

1. Ensure the full-fat cream cheese (not the spreadable type) is at room temperature, so it is soft enough to mix with the eggs easily.
2. Add one egg at a time to the cream cheese and mix together by hand or using an electric hand whisk. Mix until smooth.
3. Add all the other ingredients to the egg/cream-cheese mixture and mix slowly until a smooth batter is achieved. Do not overmix.
4. Pour into a lined loaf tin.
5. Bake at 180C/350F for 20-30 minutes, or until golden on the top and cooked in the centre.

Waffles (sweet or savoury)

Makes	Serving
5 waffles	1 waffle

Sweet waffles
Nutrition per serving: Calories: 280 | Total fat: 26g | Total carbs: 4.5g | Fibre: 2g | Sugars: 1.4g | Protein: 7g

Savoury waffles
Nutrition per serving: Calories: 323 | Total fat: 29.8g | Total carbs: 4.7g | Fibre: 2g | Sugars: 1.4g | Protein 9.4g

These make superb alternatives to sandwiches. It is helpful to make a double batch, as these waffles freeze incredibly well. Place them in an airtight container with baking parchment between each waffle. Serve sweet waffle sandwiches filled with cream cheese and berries, and savoury waffles sandwiches with ham and cheese.

Basic waffle recipe
- 5 eggs, separated
- 4 tbsp coconut flour
- 1 tsp baking powder
- 3 tbsp full-fat milk or cream
- 125g/4.5oz butter, melted

Sweet waffles – add the following:
- 3-5 tbsp granulated sweetener of choice, or more to your taste
- 1-2 tsp vanilla

Savoury waffles – add the following:
- Salt, to taste
- 1 tbsp dried herbs (I use rosemary and oregano)
- ½ cup grated/shredded cheese

First bowl
1. Whisk the egg whites until firm and forming stiff peaks.

Second bowl
1. Mix the egg yolks, coconut flour and baking powder.
2. Add the other ingredients, depending on whether you are making sweet or savoury waffles.
3. Add the melted butter slowly, mixing to ensure it is a smooth consistency.
4. Gently fold spoonfuls of the whisked egg whites into the yolk mixture. Try to keep as much of the air and fluffiness as possible.
5. Place enough of the waffle mixture into the warm waffle maker to make one waffle. Cook until golden.
6. Repeat until all the mixture has been used.

Cheesy mini loaves

Makes	Serving
12 mini loaves (or 24 small muffins)	1 mini loaf

Nutrition per serving: Calories: 170 | Total fat: 13.8g | Total carbs: 2.8g | Fibre: 1.5g | Sugars: 0.6g | Protein 6.4g

I absolutely love these. They remind me of the savoury muffins I used to enjoy at a local cafe. The trick is to add plenty of cheese to the bread mixture, and again on top. Add spring onions, pepperoni slices and pumpkin seeds to make them look like store-bought loaves and mini-muffins.

- 50g/½ cup coconut flour
- 1 tsp baking powder
- ½ spring onion, finely sliced
- 100g/1 cup grated/shredded cheese
- Salt, pepper and a pinch of chilli or rosemary to taste
- 110g/1 stick butter, melted
- 8 eggs
- Pepperoni stick, sliced to decorate
- Pumpkin seeds to decorate

1. In a large mixing bowl, add all the dry ingredients and spices. Reserve a little cheese for the topping.
2. Mix well then add the melted butter. Stir gently.
3. Add the eggs one at a time and mix after each addition. When all the eggs have been added, make sure all the ingredients are well incorporated, but do not overmix.
4. Spoon the cheesy dough into greased mini loaf tins or muffin cases.
5. To decorate, place 3 small slices of pepperoni stick along the top, sprinkle some extra pumpkin seeds, then cover with grated/shredded cheese.
6. Bake at 180C/350F for 15 minutes or until the cheese crust is golden and the centres are cooked.

oopsies

Makes	Serving
8 oopsies	1 oopsie

Nutrition per serving: Calories: 68 | Total fat: 6g | Total carbs: 0.7g | Fibre: 0g | Sugars: 0.6g | Protein 2.8g

These are the classic low-carb cloud bread. To add a little more flavour, sprinkle the tops with sesame seeds, garlic or onion flakes.

- 3 eggs
- 100g/3.5oz cream cheese
- ½ tsp baking powder
- Pinch of salt

1. Separate the egg whites into and egg yolks into two bowls.
2. Whisk the egg whites until very firm and forming soft peaks.
3. In the other bowl, add the cream cheese to the yolks and whisk until no lumps of cream cheese remain.
4. Add the baking powder and whisk again.
5. Gently fold the egg-white mixture into the egg-yolk mixture.
6. Line a baking tray with baking parchment or silicon sheet. Place large spoonfuls of oopsie batter on the tray.
7. Bake at 180C/350F for 5-10 minutes.

Recipe notes: You may add ½ tbsp psyllium husk if desired to the recipe. This will give you a sturdier, heavy bread.

Focaccia

Makes	Serving
10 slices	1 slice

Nutrition per serving: Calories: 53 | Total fat: 2.7g | Total carbs: 5.6g | Fibre: 4.2g | Sugars: 0.6g | Protein: 3.1g

I press the focaccia dough almost flat with my hands so it cooks quickly through to the centre. I also slice halfway through the focaccia before it goes in the oven, which allows it to cook evenly. Rub olive oil onto the surface and sprinkle with plenty of salt, garlic or rosemary.

- ½ cup coconut flour
- 5 tbsp psyllium husk*
- 2 tsp baking powder
- 1 tsp salt
- 4 eggs
- 250ml/1 cup boiling water

1. Place the coconut flour, psyllium husks, baking powder and salt into a large mixing bowl and stir until combined.
2. Add the eggs and mix. The mixture will be a very firm Play-Doh-like consistency, so don't work it too hard at this point.
3. Add the cup of boiling water and mix until thoroughly combined.
4. Form into a focaccia shape and place on a baking tray lined with baking parchment. Using a sharp knife, make diagonal cuts through the dough, sprinkle with plenty of salt, rosemary and place olives into the dough.
5. Bake at 180C/350F for 25-30 minutes. It is cooked when the centre is no longer spongy.
6. Serve hot with butter, or cold with cheese, avocado slices, tomatoes, etc.

Recipe notes: To ensure you avoid any eggy taste, add plenty of flavours such as rosemary, garlic, salt etc.

* Psyllium husk is 100% fibre and, once added to water, it will swell and thicken. This property is used to thicken foods, and is added to gluten-free baking where it makes these breads less crumbly. Psyllium is also used as a laxative as it retains fluid in the bowels. Always drink plenty of fluids when taking psyllium, as the husks will swell and absorb liquids from your gut as it passes through.

One-minute muffins

Makes	Serving
1 muffin	1 muffin

Nutrition per serving: Calories: 133 | Total fat: 10g | Total carbs: 3.2g | Fibre: 1.7g | Sugars: 0.9g | Protein: 7g

Many readers take a couple of attempts to get these right, so don't give up. You need to experiment with your microwave to learn how long to cook them. I know my microwave takes 45 seconds. For a savoury muffin, add cheese and a pinch of chilli. For a sweet muffin, add 1 tsp sweetener and cinnamon. Serve with melted butter and more cinnamon.

- 1 tsp butter or coconut oil
- 1 large egg
- 2 tsp coconut flour
- Pinch of baking soda
- Pinch of salt

1. Grease a ramekin dish with butter or coconut oil.
2. In a mug, mix all the ingredients together with a fork to ensure it is lump-free.
3. Place the keto muffin dough in the greased ramekin and cook in the microwave on HIGH for 1 minute. Alternatively, they can be baked in an oven, at 200C/400F for 12 minutes.
4. Cut in half and serve.

Basic bread rolls

Makes	Serving
8 bread rolls	1 bread roll

Nutrition per serving: Calories: 217 | Total fat: 16.4g | Total carbs: 11g | Fibre: 7.3g | Sugars: 1.3g | Protein: 6.1g

This basic bread rolls recipe can be adapted to make a variety of breads such as garlic bread, hamburger buns with sesame seeds, hot-dog rolls, baguettes, a simple plait or just a loaf to slice and toast. It is heavier than the basic bread loaf, so ensure you make them a little thinner than a traditional bread roll.

- 20g/¼ cup psyllium husk
- 75g/? cup coconut flour
- 1 tsp baking powder
- ½ tsp salt, or to taste
- 250ml/1 cup warm water
- 110g/ 1 stick butter, melted
- 6 eggs

1. Place all the dry ingredients in a large mixing bowl. Mix gently.
2. Add the warm water and the melted butter, and stir again.
3. Add the eggs one at a time. Mix between each additional egg.
4. Your dough will be affected by humidity, the size of the eggs and how you store your low-carb flours. If the dough is too wet, add one tablespoon of coconut flour at a time until you get the desired consistency. If too dry, add one teaspoon of warm water until it is dough-like.
5. Divide the mixture into 8 equal portions. Gently form into flat bread rolls.
6. Place on a baking tray lined with baking parchment.
7. Brush/glaze the top of each bread roll with melted butter or oil.
8. Bake at 180C/350F for 15-20 minutes, or until golden and soft.

Recipe notes:
- Because low-carb flours don't contain gluten, the dough will not be as stretchy or light as wheat-based breads.
- Low-carb dough needs to be slightly more damp than a wheat-based dough.
- Try not to overwork the dough and keep as much air as possible in the dough.
- Season well with salt, pepper, cheese or other flavours to mask any eggy or coconut flavours that some people cannot tolerate.

Three-seed bread

Makes	Serving
15 slices	1 slice

Nutrition per serving: Calories: 107 | Total fat: 8.2g | Total carbs: 5.8g | Fibre: 3.9g | Sugars: 0.4g | Protein: 3.5g

There is a famous seed loaf here in New Zealand that we have all grown up loving to eat with melted butter and Vegemite. This is as close as I can get to that traditional seed loaf, and it tastes incredible when sliced very thin, toasted, and with lots of butter dripping from it.

- 35g/¼ cup chia seeds
- 75g/½ cup sunflower seeds
- 75g/½ cup pumpkin seeds
- 25g/¼ cup coconut flour
- 75g/1 cup psyllium husks
- 1 tsp baking powder
- ¼ tsp salt
- 50g/½ stick butter, melted
- 2 eggs
- 250ml/1 cup hot water

1. Add all the dry ingredients into a mixing bowl.
2. Add the melted butter and eggs. Stir until it is almost mixed.
3. Add the cup of warm water, mix until all the ingredients are fully incorporated.
4. Place into a lined loaf tin and brush/glaze the top with oil.
5. Bake at 180C/350F for 35-45 minutes, or until golden on the top and cooked in the centre. Cooking times may vary with each oven.

If it takes you a year to get lunch boxes sorted,
then so be it.
Imagine if you started a year ago

BEEF, CHICKEN, PORK & LAMB

Meat wraps | Bunless burgers | Grain-free crumbed chicken Bacon-wrapped chicken | Beef & bacon roll-ups | Lettuce wraps (burritos) | Sausage rolls | Taco cups | Meat-lovers' Fathead pizza | Chicken "nuggets" | Mini meatloaf Pinwheels | Scotch eggs | Bacon & egg pie

Meat wraps

Nutrition will depend entirely on fillings chosen for each each wrap.

I make these every single week, without fail. I buy good-quality meat off the bone from the deli, then throw in all my children's favourite fillings. A few wraps usually disappear as I am making them – some little tummies must love them too much.

- 1 thin slice of ham, turkey or beef off the bone
- Fillings of choice – cheese, green salad, green beans, gherkins, cream cheese, sliced pepperoni, carrot sticks or tomato paste.

1. Place the thin slice of meat on the chopping board.
2. Place the fillings along the centre.
3. Roll up and secure each meat wrap with a toothpick.

Bunless burgers

Makes	Serving
5	1 burger

Nutrition per serving: Calories: 267 | Total fat: 17.1g | Total carbs: 0.1g | Fibre: 0g | Sugars: 0.1g | Protein: 26g

Bunless burgers can be served in the lunch box by placing between 2 cheese slices, 2 oopsies or 2 large mushrooms as the "buns". Place a toothpick through the centre, and why not add a gherkin, too?

- 500g/1lb ground/minced beef
- 1 egg
- Salt and pepper to taste
- ½ red onion, finely diced (optional)

1. If adding a diced red onion, pre-cook it by frying in a little butter until soft then add to a bowl with the ground/minced beef.
2. Now add the egg and seasoning. Mix with hands until well combined.
3. Divide the mixture into 5 portions. Take each portion of ground/minced beef, and squeeze it into a firm, flat burger shape. The firmer you squeeze it into shape, the more likely it is to stay together while cooking.
4. Fry gently until thoroughly cooked on both sides.

Grain-free crumbed chicken

Makes	Serving
6 drumsticks	1 drumstick

Nutrition per serving: Calories: 404 | Total fat: 31g | Total carbs: 3.5g | Fibre: 2g | Sugars: 0.7g | Protein: 27.7g

These healthy little crumbed chicken drumsticks are everything you ever want in a piece of fried chicken, only without the grains and unhealthy oils. What makes them even better? There is almost zero washing up as they are prepared in a disposable food bag. You can also use this coating recipe for chicken wings, thighs or breast.

- 6 chicken drumsticks, skin on
- 100g/1 cup almond meal/flour
- ½ tsp ginger powder
- ½ tsp dried parsley
- 1 tsp paprika
- ¼ tsp chilli powder
- ½ tsp dried sage
- ½ tsp mustard powder
- ¼ tsp Chinese five spice
- ½ tsp dried basil
- Salt and pepper to taste

1. Put the ground almonds and all the herbs and spices into a plastic food bag, twist or zip the top and shake to mix.
2. Open the bag and add the chicken drumsticks, twist/zip the top, shake and rub the mixture through the bag onto the chicken.
3. In a baking dish, add 1-2ml olive oil.
4. Place the chicken drumsticks on the oiled baking dish.
5. Spray or brush with oil and bake at 180C/350F for 45 minutes.
6. Turn 2 or 3 times while they are cooking, so all the coating gets covered in the olive oil.

Bacon-wrapped chicken

Makes	Serving
5 portions	2 pieces

Nutrition per serving: Calories: 230 | Total fat: 9.6g | Total carbs: 0.3g | Fibre: 0g | Sugars: 0.1g | Protein: 32.2g

Now who doesn't like something wrapped in bacon? It just tastes so good. Make extra, as I'm sure you will want to enjoy some of these as well.

Bacon-wrapped chicken nuggets
- 10 pieces chicken tenderloins or strips
- 10 slices streaky bacon

Sauce (optional)
- 50g/2oz cream cheese
- Double/heavy cream – add enough to deglaze the pan and make a sauce

1. Wrap each chicken tenderloin with a slice of streaky bacon.
2. These can be cooked two ways. Either place in a baking dish and bake at 180C/350F for 20 minutes, or gently fry in a frying pan for 15 minutes until golden on all sides and cooked throughout.
3. Remove the bacon-wrapped chicken then add the cream cheese to deglaze the baking dish or frying pan. This will add the bacon flavour into the cream cheese to make a beautiful creamy sauce. Add enough double/heavy cream to make the sauce as pourable as you like it.

Beef & bacon roll-ups

Nutrition values cannot be given as your beef and bacon will vary in thickness and therefore weight. Needless to say, this is pretty much carb-free apart from the spinach (1g net carbs per 100g) and cheese (negligible, depending on the cheese). Nutritional values will also vary according to how thick you cut each beef and bacon roll-up.

So, so easy; so, so tasty; and so, so versatile. Beef and bacon roll-ups can be served as a single roll, or sliced as shown into little sushi-like pieces – perfect for little hands to hold.

- 4 steaks beef schnitzel
- 4 slices streaky bacon
- Handful of spinach
- Cheese of choice

1. Lay the beef schnitzel on a chopping board. Place the streaky bacon along the length of the beef.
2. Place some leafy greens on top of the streaky bacon. Add your favourite cheese across the meat. This will become the centre.
3. Roll the beef and the fillings up tightly. Secure with a toothpick if required.
4. Place each beef and bacon roll up in a baking dish or baking tray. Spray or brush with oil.
5. Cook at 180C/350F for approximately 15-20 minutes until the beef and bacon are cooked thoroughly. Cooking time will depend on the thickness of your beef and bacon, so may vary widely.
6. Serve hot with mushroom sauce or allow to completely cool, then using a sharp knife, carefully cut into small slices as shown.

Lettuce wraps (burritos)

Makes	Serving
6 lettuce wraps	1 lettuce wrap

Nutrition per serving: Calories: 235 | Total fat: 14g | Total carbs: 4.3g | Fibre: 1.5g | Sugars: 2.5g | Protein: 22g

Lettuce wraps can be easy to hold, especially if you use two lettuce leaves to truly wrap all the fillings in place. I have a rectangular container which fits one lettuce wrap in tightly, so it arrives at school in one piece. Alternatively, you can wrap each one with baking paper, and tie with some string or ribbon.

- 1 onion, quartered then sliced
- 2 cloves garlic, crushed
- 500g/1lb ground/minced beef
- 1 tbsp ground cumin
- 1 tsp ground chilli
- 1 tbsp dried coriander
- 400g/14oz tinned/canned/freshly diced tomato

1. Heat oil in a saucepan and gently fry the onion and garlic until cooked.
2. Add the mince/ground beef and continue to cook and stir until the meat is browned and cooked.
3. Add the herbs, spices and tomatoes. Stir thoroughly.
4. Simmer and stir occasionally for 15 minutes until the sauce has thickened and all the meat is thoroughly cooked.
5. Allow to cool and keep in an airtight container in the fridge until morning.
6. Place some cooked beef mix in the lettuce leaves. Add plenty of capsicum/bell-pepper slices, avocado, grated/shredded cheese and other favourite burrito ingredients, such as sour cream. Wrap firmly in the lettuce leaf.
7. Secure with a toothpick, string, ribbon or place in a rectangular container.

No avocado or sour cream has been included in the nutrition panel, as how much you add is up to each individual.

Sausage rolls

Makes	Serving
6	Sixth of recipe (see below)

Nutrition per serving: Calories: 470 | Total fat: 39.1g | Total carbs: 5.1g | Fibre: 1.5g | Sugars: 1.9g | Protein: 26g

The sausage rolls you may find in the supermarket or bakery are often made with trans fats and the sausage is packed with starchy fillers, such as rice flour or wheat. Choose the best sausages you can with the highest percentage of meat and the lowest percentage of carbs.

Sausage rolls
- 500g/1lb sausages
- Onion flakes to garnish

Pastry
- 170g/6oz/1¾ cups pre-grated/shredded mozzarella or Edam/mild cheese
- 85g/3oz/¾ cup almond meal/flour
- 2 tbsp full-fat cream cheese
- 1 egg
- Pinch of salt, to taste
- 1 tsp onion flakes

Recipe notes: The sausage-roll pastry can also be made by replacing the almond meal/flour with ¼ cup (4 tbsp) coconut flour.

The nutrition panel is per serving (the entire recipe makes 6 servings). The number of sausage rolls you make will depend on how big or small you cut them.

Nutrition calculated using pork sausages containing 1.5% carbs.

Pre-cook the sausages
1. Cut the sausage casing down the centre using a sharp knife. Peel back the casing and discard.
2. Place each sausage on a lined baking tray and cook at 180C/350F for 10 minutes.

Pastry
1. While the sausages are cooking, prepare the pastry.
2. Mix the grated/shredded cheese and almond meal/flour in a microwaveable bowl. Add the cream cheese. Microwave on HIGH for 1 minute. Alternatively, melt the cheeses together gently in a saucepan on the stove top.
3. Stir then microwave on HIGH for another 30 seconds. Remove and stir again. Add the egg, salt, and onion flakes. Mix.
4. Place the pastry between two pieces of baking parchment/paper and roll into a thin rectangle. Remove the top piece of baking paper/parchment.
5. Cut the pastry along one side and place the sausages along that edge. Begin to roll the pastry over the cooked sausages and cut off the excess pastry.
6. Cut into small or medium sized sausage rolls and spray or drizzle oil over the top. Sprinkle with onion flakes (or sesame seeds) to garnish.
7. Bake at 220C/425F for 12-15 minutes, or until golden all over.

Taco cups

Makes	Serving
5 taco cups	1 taco cup

Nutrition per serving: Calories: 511 | Total fat: 35.6g | Total carbs: 9.7g | Fibre: 3.6g | Sugars: 4.2g | Protein: 38.4g

All children love eating these with their hands. Place each taco cup in the lunch box with cheese and send a little pot of sour cream or salsa to pour on top when it's lunchtime. I make these for dinner and save the leftovers especially for lunch boxes.

Beef mix
- 1 onion, sliced
- 500g/1lb ground/minced beef
- 400g/14oz tinned/canned tomatoes, diced
- ½ tsp chilli powder
- 1 tbsp tomato paste

Taco cups
- 170g/6oz/1¾ cups pre-grated/shredded mozzarella or Edam/mild cheese
- 85g/3oz/¾ cup almond meal/flour
- 2 tbsp full-fat cream cheese
- 1 egg
- Pinch of salt, to taste
- 1 tsp cumin powder
- 1 tsp coriander/cilantro powder
- Pinch of chilli powder

Beef mix
1. Gently fry the diced onion in oil until clear then add the meat, breaking it up into tiny pieces as it cooks and browns. This should take up to 5 minutes.
2. Add the spices and tinned/canned tomato and tomato paste. Stir then simmer on a low heat for 15 minutes (uncovered, to thicken the meat sauce) while you make the taco cups and side salad.

Taco cups
1. Mix the grated/shredded cheese and almond meal/flour in a microwaveable bowl. Add the cream cheese. Microwave on HIGH for 1 minute. Alternatively, you may melt these together gently in a saucepan on the stove top.
2. Stir then microwave on HIGH for another 30 seconds. Remove and stir again. Add the egg, salt, and spices. Mix.
3. Place the taco pastry between two pieces of baking parchment/paper and roll into a thin, rectangle. Remove the top baking paper/parchment.
4. Cut the taco pastry into circles using a cookie cutter or a glass tumbler (I managed to make 15 taco cups). Place each one on

To serve (optional)
- Green side salad
- Guacamole
- Salsa
- Pre-grated/shredded mozzarella
- Avocado
- Sour cream

an upside-down, oiled muffin tray OR individual silicone muffin cases. Then bake at 220C/425F for 12-15 minutes, or until browned on the top.

5. Remove each taco cup, place on a baking tray lined with baking parchment/paper and bake again for 2 minutes to allow the inside to brown and crisp slightly.

To make the taco cups
1. Place the keto taco cups on a serving plate and load up with the cooked beef mix.
2. Add cheese, salsa, guacamole and cheese. Reheat if you like the cheese melted.
3. Serve with sour cream and a green side salad with plenty of oil or dressing.

Recipe notes: Taco pastry can also be made by replacing the almond meal/flour with ¼ cup (4 tbsp) coconut flour.

Nutrition notes were calculated using the taco cups and cooked beef mix sauce divided equally between 5 servings. Extra toppings will be additional, because what and how much you use will be completely different for everyone.

Meat-lovers' Fathead pizza

Makes	Serving
1 pizza	1 slice

Nutrition per serving: Calories: 203 | Total fat: 16.8g | Total carbs: 4g | Fibre: 1.6g | Sugars: 1g | Protein: 11g

There are endless variations for a classic meat-lovers' Fathead pizza. Allow your child to add their own favourite toppings, so you can guarantee it will be eaten. Why not press two slices together to make a meat-lovers' sandwich?

Topping suggestions

Pizza sauces
- Tomato paste (check for no added sugars)
- Pesto
- Olive tapenade

Meats
For all meats, choose the least processed, with the highest meat contents, and those that has not been cured with sugar, honey, wheat or other grains. Choose meat from the bone and stay away from pre-formed meat.
- Ham, off the bone
- Bacon
- Pepperoni
- Salami
- Biersticks
- Ground/minced beef, chicken or pork
- Diced sausage
- Smoked chicken
- Pastrami
- Chorizo

Cheeses
- Mozzarella
- Parmesan
- Cheddar
- Mild
- Colby
- Edam
- Blue cheese
- Camembert
- Brie
- Ricotta
- Gruyère
- Goats' cheese
- Feta

Herbs and spices
- Chilli
- Rosemary

- Oregano
- Thyme

Vegetables and greenery
- Thinly sliced onions
- Garlic
- Basil
- Spring onions
- Mushrooms
- Chives
- Mint
- Bell peppers
- Olives
- Sun-dried tomatoes
- Avocado
- Fennel
  - 170g/6oz/1¾ cups pre-grated/shredded cheese. Mozzarella is the best, or Edam/mild cheese
  - 85g/3oz/¾ cup almond meal/flour (see recipe notes below)
  - 2 tbsp cream cheese
  - 1 egg
  - Pinch of salt to taste
  - Herbs and spices
  - Choice of meats and toppings

1. Mix the grated/shredded cheese and almond meal/flour (or coconut flour, if using) in a microwaveable bowl. Add the cream cheese. Microwave on HIGH for 1 minute. Alternatively you may melt the cheeses together gently in a saucepan on the stove top.
2. Stir, then microwave on HIGH for further 30 seconds.
3. Add the egg, salt, herbs, spices or flavourings, and mix gently.
4. Place in between two pieces of baking parchment and roll into a circular pizza shape. Remove the top baking parchment.
5. Make fork holes all over the pizza base to ensure it cooks evenly.
6. Slide the baking parchment with the pizza base, on a baking tray (cookie tray) or pizza stone, and bake at 220C/425F for 12-15 minutes, or until brown.
7. To make the base really crispy and sturdy, flip the pizza over onto baking parchment)once the top has browned.
8. Once cooked, remove from the oven and add all the sauces, meat and toppings you like. Make sure any meat you use is already cooked, as this time it goes back into the oven just to heat and melt the cheese. Bake again at 220C/425F for 5 minutes.

Recipe notes: Low-carb pizza pastry can also be made by replacing the almond meal/flour with 1/4 cup (4 tbsp) coconut flour.

Nutrition panel is for the pizza base only. The nutrition for the toppings will vary widely, depending on which meat is used, which vegetables or sauces were chosen, and the quantity used. I have never seen two meat-lovers' pizzas the same.

Chicken "nuggets"

Makes	Serving
6	Sixth of recipe

Nutrition per serving: Calories: 443 | Total fat: 25.5g| Total carbs: 4.5g | Fibre: 2g | Sugars: 0.8g | Protein: 49g

Avoid all processed chicken nuggets like the plague. They are generally made with chicken bits and pieces, then packed together with cheap, starchy fillers. They are then fried in unhealthy oils. This recipe is made with 100% chicken breast with a light coating of almond meal or coconut flour. They taste incredible.

First bowl
- 1 egg, beaten
- 4 tbsp oil

Second bowl
- 850g/1.9lb chicken breast
- 100g/1 cup almond meal/flour or ½ cup coconut flour
- ½ tsp salt
- ½ tsp garlic powder
- 1 tsp onion flakes

First bowl
1. Mix the egg and oil together with a fork.

Second bowl
1. Mix the almond or coconut flour, salt, garlic and onion together.
2. Cut the chicken breast into strips or nugget-sized pieces. Dip each one in the egg/oil mixture, then dip it in the coating and cover fully.
3. Fry each chicken nugget in oil on both sides, until golden and cooked thoroughly in the centre.
4. Alternatively, you can bake these on a lined baking tray at 180C/350F for 10-15 minutes.
5. Serve with salsa, sugar-free tomato sauce or garlic mayonnaise.

Mini meatloaf

Makes	Serving
12	1 mini meatloaf

Nutrition per serving: Calories: 221 | Total fat: 17.2g | Total carbs: 1g | Fibre: 0.4g | Sugars: 0.7g | Protein: 15.2g

These are the perfect way to disguise hidden vegetables, especially if you shred/grate the vegetables first. Add plenty of cheese as a crusty topping. Yum!

Base recipe
- 1 onion, finely diced
- 700g/1.5lb ground/minced beef, turkey or pork
- 2 eggs, lightly beaten
- Salt and pepper to taste
- 100g/3.5oz grated/shredded cheese

Examples of flavourings
- 2 slices bacon, diced
- Handful of fresh basil
- Handful of fresh parsley
- ¼ cup sundried tomatoes, diced
- 2 tsp dried oregano

1. Mix the diced onion, meat, eggs and salt and pepper together.
2. Add your choice of seasonings and flavourings. I have given one example, but take a look below for a huge range of ideas.
3. Mix all the ingredients together with your hands and place a small handful of the meatloaf mixture into muffin trays. Press gently, not too hard, otherwise they will turn into meatballs.
4. Cover with the grated cheese, and sprinkle with grated parmesan if desired.
5. Cook at 180C/350F.

Italian: add garlic, oregano, Italian seasoning, rosemary and basil
Mexican: add coriander (cilantro), cumin, chilli and capsicums/bell peppers, and serve with avocado and salsa
Cheeseburger meatloaf: add mustard, hide cheese inside which will melt when cooked, and serve with homemade ketchup
Toppings: grated/shredded cheese, bacon pieces or slices, Parmesan, mozzarella, sliced tomato covered in cheese
Perhaps hide these inside: organ meat, grated carrot, finely diced mushrooms, celery, grated zucchini or chopped spinach

Pinwheels

My secret to making anything look cute and attractive to a child is good, old-fashioned toothpicks. Most parents use them for quick and easy party finger food, so why not utilise them in the lunch box, too? They don't take any extra time, but just look how adorable they make the lunch box appear.

- **Meat wraps**: thinly sliced meat such as ham, beef, turkey, chicken or pepperoni
- **Vegetables wraps**: lettuce, thinly sliced zucchini/courgette, carrots, or wilted cabbage
- **Spreads**: spreadable cream cheese, "traffic light dips" (see page 89), avocado or cottage cheese
- **Fillings**: tuna in olive oil or mayonnaise, grated/shredded cheese, grated/shredded carrots, salad, shredded chicken etc

1. Place your wrap onto the chopping board.
2. Spread the wrap with your choice of spread.
3. Add fillings and roll up gently.
4. Place toothpicks along the length and cut into small pieces, or cut into small pieces then place each one onto a long bamboo skewer.

Scotch eggs

Makes	Serving
6 Scotch eggs	1 Scotch egg

Nutrition per serving: Calories: 169 | Total fat: 8.2g | Total carbs: 0.7g | Fibre: 0g | Sugars: 0.5g | Protein: 23.1g

Optional toppings for extra flavour, sprinkle some Parmesan, onion flakes or sesame seeds over each Scotch egg. These are little powerhouses of protein.

- 6 eggs
- 500g/1lb ground/minced pork, beef or lamb
- 2 tsp herb or spice of choice, such as sage, curry powder, rosemary, parsley or mustard
- ½ tsp salt to taste
- Onion flakes to garnish (optional)

1. Place eggs in a saucepan of cold water and bring to the boil. Boil for 4 minutes. Drain the hot water from the saucepan, then immediately cover the eggs in cold water so they will be cool enough to be peeled.
2. Peel the eggs and pat dry with kitchen paper. This will let the ground/minced meat to stick to the egg more easily.
3. Mix the ground/minced meat with your chosen herbs and spices.
4. Use a small handful of the ground/minced meat and flatten it in your hand, appearing like a very thin hamburger patty. Place the egg onto the meat and slowly work the meat around the egg ensuring you completely cover the egg.
5. Place all the Scotch eggs in an oiled baking tray, and cook for 30 minutes at 180C/350F.

Recipe notes: For most recipes, I use high-fat meats, but Paleo Scotch eggs hold together better if you use lean meat, otherwise the fat melts out and the pork casing may split.

Low-carb lunches: How to make real-food lunch boxes | 75

Bacon & egg pie

Makes	Serving
6	1 slice

Nutrition per serving: Calories: 201 | Total fat: 17.7g | Total carbs: 1.6g | Fibre: 0g | Sugars: 1.4g | Protein: 18g

A crustless bacon and egg pie is one of the quickest lunch-box fillers you can make. Turn the oven on and, by the time it is up to temperature, you will have prepared the ingredients, and it will be ready to be cooked.

- 8 eggs
- 130ml/½ cup full-fat milk or cream
- 1 spring onion, finely sliced
- 2 slices bacon, diced
- 100g/3.5oz/1 cup grated/shredded cheese
- Salt and pepper to taste
- Grated/shredded cheese to garnish

1. Whisk the eggs and milk with a fork.
2. Add all the other ingredients, reserving the extra cheese for the topping.
3. Add any vegetables you wish and stir gently.
4. Pour into a 20cm/8-inch square baking dish that has been greased and lined with baking parchment.
5. You may need to move the vegetables in the dish with the fork so they are evenly distributed.
6. Place the extra cheese on top.
7. Bake at 180C/350F for 20-30 minutes.

Recipe notes: The nutritional values are calculated on the recipe without added vegetables. You will have to calculate the vegetable values depending on what and how much you add to the pie.

Stop the snacking – it only creates picky kids who won't eat at mealtimes

MEAT-FREE DISHES

Egg wraps | Courgette, feta & mint fritters | Salmon quiche
Boiled eggs & cheese soldiers | Spinach & feta flan
Smoked-salmon sushi | Tuna fishcakes

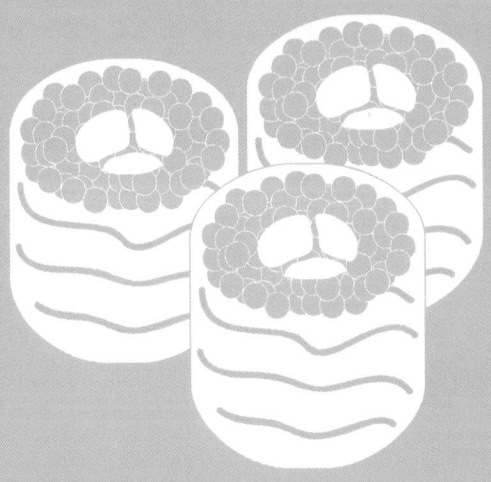

Egg Wraps

Makes	Serving
1 wrap	1 wrap

Nutrition per serving: Calories: 192 | Total fat: 18.7g | Total carbs: 0.4g | Fibre: 0g | Sugars: 0.4g | Protein: 5.5g

Egg wraps are a great alternative to wheat wraps, and you can flavour them any way you like. Make sure they are cold before you add any salad fillings, or add cheese while they are warm so it melts across the entire wrap.

- 1 egg per wrap
- 1 tbsp coconut oil or butter
- Salt and pepper to taste

1. Whisk the egg in a bowl until there are no lumps and you cannot see any egg yolk/white pieces.
2. Heat some coconut oil or butter in a frying pan.
3. Pour the egg mixture into the frying pan and rotate the pan to let the egg spread out into a very thin layer.
4. Once cooked on one side, flip over.
5. Remove each wrap as they cook and leave on a plate to allow to cool.
6. Repeat with as many eggs as you like until you have made enough wraps for the next few days.
7. Place your favourite filling inside and roll up.

Courgette, feta & mint fritters

Makes	Serving
5 fritters	1 fritter

Nutrition per serving: Calories: 80 | Total fat: 4.5g | Total carbs: 5.5g | Fibre: 1.5g | Sugars: 4g | Protein: 5.5g

Buy courgettes/zucchini when they are in season, and make a large batch of this recipe for the week ahead. Many fritters have wheat, flour or other agents to bind them together. You don't need any of these – just four ingredients go into these low-carb fritters.

- 4-5 courgettes/zucchini, grated/shredded
- 50g/½ cup feta, cut into cubes
- 1 handful of fresh mint, roughly chopped
- 2 eggs

1. Grate/shred the courgette/zucchini and squeeze out all the excess water.
2. Add the mint, feta and eggs and stir through.
3. Heat a frying pan and add fry small batches in coconut oil or butter until golden.

Top tip: To prevent your fritters from becoming soggy, ensure you have squeezed out every drop of water from the grated/shredded courgette/zucchini. Also, don't add salt to the mixture – that draws out even more water and can actually make them soggier. Instead, season them with salt at the dinner table. The egg has a tendency to drain to the bottom of the mixing bowl, so stir the mixture each time before you add another spoonful to the frying pan.

Salmon quiche

Serves	Serving
10	1 slice

Nutrition per serving: Calories: 207 | Total fat: 16.2g | Total carbs: 2.2g | Fibre: 0g | Sugars: 1.7g | Protein: 17.2g

This is such an economical way to make an expensive piece of salmon stretch for a family. You may want to bake it in mini muffin tins or cupcake cases ready for school lunches or a handy, high-protein snack.

- 500g/1lb salmon fillet, diced/cubed
- 8 eggs
- 250g/8.8oz full-fat cream cheese, diced/cubed
- 250ml/1 cup full-fat milk or cream
- Pinch of salt and pepper to taste
- 1 tsp dried dill

1. Whisk the eggs with a fork.
2. Whisk in the milk, salt, pepper and dill.
3. Add the diced salmon and cream cheese.
4. Mix gently with a fork.
5. Pour into a greased, lined dish. Move the pieces of salmon around until they are evenly distributed.
6. Bake at 180C/350F for 30 minutes.

Boiled eggs & cheese soldiers

Serves	Serving
1	1 egg with cheese soldiers

Nutrition per serving: Calories: 271 | Total fat: 21.5g | Total carbs: 1.1g | Fibre: 0g | Sugars: 0.6g | Protein: 17.6g

This is such a cute lunch-box filler, and perfect for a warm, hearty breakfast. Everyone loves the simplicity of this recipe and says: "Why didn't I think of this? Genius!"

- 1 egg
- 50g/1.8oz full-fat cheese, cut into sticks (soldiers)

1. Place your egg in a saucepan of cold water, cover with a lid and bring the water and eggs to the boil.
2. Once the water is really boiling and bubbling away, turn the heat off, and place the saucepan (with the water and eggs) to rest away from the heat.
3. Set your timer and leave your eggs in the saucepan of hot water for the following times:
   Soft and runny centre = 4 minutes
   Semi soft centre = 6 minutes
   Medium = 10 minutes
   Hard boiled = 16 minutes
4. Once your eggs are cooked for the required time, drain the water immediately and serve hot with a cheese soldier. Alternatively, run under cold water and, once completely cold, keep in the fridge.

Spinach & feta flan

Serves	Serving
15	1 triangle

Nutrition per serving: Calories: 129 | Total fat: 9.4g | Total carbs: 2.4g | Fibre: 1g | Sugars: 1.1g | Protein: 9.1g

A crustless spinach and feta flan is a brilliant way to get more greens into your children. The secret is the mint and feta, which makes them irresistible. And because the flan is crustless, the recipe is quick, easy and grain-free.

- 1 spring onion, finely sliced
- 400g/14oz spinach, fresh or frozen
- 12 eggs, beaten
- 200g/7oz feta, crumbled
- A huge handful of fresh mint, chopped
- Salt and pepper to taste
- 100g/1 cup grated/shredded cheese for the cheesy crust

1. If using frozen spinach, defrost then squeeze as much of the water out as you can. This is an important step, otherwise you will end up with a soggy pie. If using fresh spinach, dice the leaves into small pieces.
2. Place the spinach and all other ingredients in a large mixing bowl.
3. Mix gently, but try to leave some visible lumps of feta.
4. Pour the mixture onto an oiled and lined baking dish.
5. Sprinkle the grated/shredded cheese over the top.
6. Bake at 180C/350F for 30-40 minutes, or until the centre is cooked.

Smoked-salmon sushi

Serves	Serving
4	¼ recipe

Nutrition per serving: Calories: 160 | Total fat: 10g | Total carbs: 0.9g | Fibre: 0g | Sugars: 0.9g | Protein: 16.9g

If you and your children love sushi, but have now realised they are not much more than starchy rice, sweet vinegar and a smattering of salmon, then these are the perfect antidote.

- 100g/3.5oz smoked-salmon slices
- 100g/3.5oz spreadable cream cheese

1. Place the smoked salmon on the chopping board or plate.
2. Gently spread the spreadable cream cheese along one length.
3. Roll up then cut into sushi-sized slices.
4. Place a toothpick in each to prevent the salmon sushi from unrolling.

Tuna fishcakes

Makes	Serving
10 fish cakes	2 fish cakes

Nutrition per serving: Calories: 208 | Total fat: 12.4g | Total carbs: 4.2g | Fibre: 2.7g | Sugars: 0.7g | Protein: 18.2g

These tasty little fishcakes can be baked in the oven or made in the frying pan. And if you children don't like tuna? No problem. Use fresh salmon instead.

- 300g/10oz tinned/canned tuna in olive oil
- 3 eggs
- 4 tbsp coconut flour (see notes)
- 1 tbsp curry powder
- Salt/pepper to taste

1. Do not drain the canned/tinned tuna in olive oil. Place the tuna and olive oil into a mixing bowl.
2. Add all the other ingredients and mix well until the coconut flour begins to thicken.
3. Add more coconut flour if required (see recipe notes). The mixture will be quite oily, but as long as you can squeeze it into a ball, it will cook beautifully and not dry out. Do not over-thicken the recipe.
4. Press a small amount of the tuna fishcake mixture into your hand and squeeze to form a ball. Gently from it into a fishcake/patty shape with your fingers.
5. Fry in oil until crispy on both sides, or bake at 180C/350F for 15 minutes, turning once.
6. Keep in an airtight container in the fridge for up to three days.

Recipe notes: I buy tuna (70%) in olive oil. Check your brand contains olive oil only, not an olive-oil blend, otherwise it will contain seed oils such as sunflower or canola. Each brand will contain more or less oil, so you may need an extra tablespoon of coconut flour to ensure the fishcakes set. frying pan.

SNACK & SAUCES

Parmesan crisps | Pork crackling | Traffic lights

Parmesan crisps

Serves	Serving
16	1 Parmesan crisp

Nutrition per serving: Calories: 26 | Total fat: 1.7g | Total carbs: 0.8g | Fibre: 0g | Sugars: 0g | Protein: 1.8g

Your children may miss their usual crackers made with wheat and grains, and still crave that crunch. These are perfect – so easy to make. Add your child's favourite herbs and spices.

- 1 cup/100g grated/shredded Parmesan cheese
- Herbs or spices such as garlic, chilli, rosemary or cracked pepper to taste

1. Mix the grated/shredded Parmesan with the herbs or spices.
2. Place small rounds on a parchment-lined baking sheet. I use a circular cookie-cutter to get a perfect round shape. Allow enough room for each Parmesan crisp to melt and spread while cooking.
3. Alternatively, you can spread the entire mixture in one layer and bake until crisp, then snap into pieces, or use a pizza-cutting wheel to slice into squares.
4. Bake at 180C/350F for 4–8 minutes or until golden.
5. Remove from the oven and allow to cool on the lined baking sheet, or remove and place over an upside-down oiled muffin tin to create Parmesan cups.

Low-carb lunches: How to make real-food lunch boxes | 87

Pork crackling

Nutrition per 100g: Calories: 529 | Total fat: 35.3g | Total carbs: 0g | Fibre: 0g | Sugars: 0g | Protein: 49.4g

This is a super-crunchy snack that is high in protein and gives that salty taste that so many children love in processed snacks.

- Sheets of pork skin/crackling
- Oil of your choice (I like coconut)
- Salt
- Herbs or spices

1. Place the pork skin/crackling on an oiled baking tray with a 1-inch lip to stop any oil running off the tray. Season with salt and/or herbs and spices.
2. Cook at 180C/350F for 10 minutes until soft.
3. Remove from the oven and using kitchen tongs and kitchen scissors, cut into strips or shapes.
4. Cook until golden and crispy.
5. Drain the melted pork fat into a heatproof jug.
6. Cool the melted fat and use for cooking lard. Store the lard in the fridge – it's a wonderful, stable cooking fat, full of flavour.

Traffic lights

It is so important to serve dips to children to help the transition to low-carb, real food. Don't worry – you may not need to be so creative later on, but at the beginning it may just be the sauce that wins them over. Sauces can make your child's lunch box more colourful and fun.

Red light
This is just regular salsa. When you buy salsa, make sure you check for added sugar, seed oils or thickeners. Find the best one you can, with the fewest ingredients. You can make salsa yourself, but children seem to find the store-bought varieties far more acceptable and as close to ketchup as they will tolerate at the beginning.

Orange light
Dice orange capsicums/bell peppers and place them in a blender with full-fat cream cheese. Pulse until smooth and there are no lumps. As your child grows to like this, allow more lumps to appear. One thing fussy kids suffer from is the avoidance of lumps or visual pieces of food in a dish. Once you get over this stumbling block, many more battles will be won. I know adults who still avoid lumps. You don't want your child to be that adult.

Green light
We call this one "slime" in our house. Boys especially love grossing out their friends by eating slime at lunch. Simply mash a ripe avocado with spreadable cream cheese and a little lemon juice. Lemon juice prevents the avocado from browning in their lunch box. Alternatively, stir pesto through spreadable cream cheese. A caution for those with nut allergies: many pestos contain nuts, especially cashews.

SWEET BAKING

Chocolate zucchini cake | Coconut-flour cupcakes — three ways | Paleo seed bars | Chocolate cookies | Blueberry triangles | Blueberry paleo pancakes | Chelsea buns | Carrot cupcakes | Coconut flour chocolate-chip cookies

Chocolate Zucchini cake

Makes	Serving
10 large slices	1 slice

Nutrition per serving: Calories: 407 | Total fat: 39g | Total carbs: 9.6g | Fibre: 4.4g | Sugars: 3.2g | Protein: 9.5g

This is a sneaky way to get more greens into picky kids. You can even peel the zucchini/courgettes to make them disappear within the cake.

- 220g/8oz/2 sticks butter, softened
- 3-5 tbsp granulated sweetener of choice, or more to your taste
- 2 tsp vanilla essence or paste
- 5 medium eggs
- 200g/7oz/2 cup almond meal/flour
- 2 tsp baking powder
- 45g/1.5oz/½ cup unsweetened cocoa powder
- 4 cups grated/shredded zucchini/courgettes, loosely packed. After you have measured the 4 cups, squeeze out most of the liquid so the cake isn't soggy

1. Place the softened butter, sweetener and vanilla in a mixing bowl and mix until smooth.
2. Add the eggs one by one, mixing in between each egg.
3. Add the almond meal/flour, baking powder and cocoa. Mix until smooth.
4. Stir in the grated/shredded zucchini/courgette and mix gently until it is hidden within the chocolate-cake mixture.
5. Divide the mixture between two sandwich baking tins which have been oiled and lined.
6. Bake at 180C/350F for 25–30 minutes until completely cooked in the centre.
7. Once cooled, serve with whipped cream between each layer and on top. Decorate with chopped strawberries.

Coconut-flour cupcakes — three ways

Makes	Serving
12 basic cupcakes (flavours are in addition)	1 basic cupcake

Nutrition per serving: Calories: 130 | Total fat: 11g | Total carbs: 3.1g | Fibre: 1.6g | Sugars: 0.7g | Protein: 4.3g

Of all my sweet recipes, this is probably my favourite because it is so adaptable. It is also nut-free, so perfect for those who attend nut-free schools. I use it as my basic sponge and cupcake recipe and vary the fillings.

- 110g/1 stick/4oz butter, melted
- ½ cup coconut flour
- 3-5 tbsp granulated sweetener of choice, or more to your taste
- 1 tsp baking powder
- 8 eggs

1. Mix together the melted butter, coconut flour, sweetener and baking powder until smooth.
2. Add the eggs one by one, mixing in between each addition.
3. Add any additional flavours that are required into the cupcake batter.
4. Spoon the mixture evenly between 12 cupcake cases.
5. Bake at 180C/350F for 10-15 minutes until cooked in the centre.

Vanilla cupcakes: add 2 tsp vanilla

Lemon-drizzle cupcakes: add 2 tbsp lemon zest to cupcake batter. Squeeze lemon juice into a glass and dissolve some sweetener into the juice. Drizzle over the top of each cupcake when still warm.

Blueberry cupcakes: add 2 tsp vanilla and ½ cup frozen blueberries. Frozen blueberries stops the cupcake batter from turning purple.

Paleo seed bars

Makes	Serving
22 bars	1 seed bar

Nutrition per serving: Calories: 151 | Total fat: 13.5g | Total carbs: 5.1g | Fibre: 3.1g | Sugars: 0.7g | Protein: 5.2g

These seed bars are perfect for schools that have a nut-free policy. Why not drizzle them with 90% chocolate to make them appear like store-bought bars? Store-bought granola/muesli bars appear to be healthy, but contain an astounding amount of sugar. Avoid bars which contain dried fruit – they're sugar-dense and have very little nutritional value.

- 300g/10.5oz seeds of choice
- 50g/1.8oz ground flaxseed/linseed
- 3 eggs
- 50g/1.8oz coconut oil
- 2 tsp vanilla extract
- 2 tsp ground cinnamon
- 4 tbsp granulated sweetener of choice, or more to your taste
- 4 tbsp cocoa nibs
- 100g/1 cup shredded/desiccated coconut, unsweetened
- 30g/⅓ cup cocoa powder, unsweetened

1. Place the seeds, linseed and eggs in the food processor with the blade attachment. Pulse until the seeds are roughly chopped and mixed with the eggs.
2. Place all the other ingredients in the food-processor bowl and pulse until thoroughly mixed and starting to clump together.
3. Pour the seed-bar mix into a baking dish (17x25cm/7x10-inch internal measurements), lined with baking parchment.
4. Press very firmly into the baking dish to ensure the seed bars are solid and not crumbly when they are cooked.
5. Bake at 180C/350F for 15-20 minutes until baked and slightly crisp.
6. Allow to cool. Cut into 22 seed bars.

Chocolate cookies

Makes	Serving
14 cookies	1 cookie

Nutrition per serving: Calories: 217 | Total fat: 20.3g | Total carbs: 6.7g | Fibre: 4g | Sugars: 1.8g | Protein: 4.9g

Ask your child to help your decorate these cookies with dark chocolate. Drizzle them, dip them or just spoon the dark chocolate over the top. You can even add pieces of walnuts inside the cookies if you like nutty cookies.

- 55g/½ stick butter, softened
- 4 tbsp cocoa, unsweetened
- 2 tbsp granulated sweetener of choice, or more to your taste
- 100g/1 cup shredded/desiccated coconut, unsweetened
- 2 eggs
- 200g/2 cups almond meal/flour
- Pinch of salt

1. Mix the softened butter, sweetener and cocoa together until smooth.
2. Add all other ingredients and mix well.
3. Roll mixture into 14 small balls, then place on a baking tray lined with baking parchment. Press each cookie gently with a fork.
4. Bake at 180C/350F for 15-20 minutes.

Blueberry triangles

Makes	Serving
12 triangles	1 triangle

Nutrition per serving: Calories: 139 | Total fat: 11.1g | Total carbs: 5.3g | Fibre: 2.1g | Sugars: 2.3g | Protein: 4.3g

Another fail-safe recipe to help curb those sweet cravings. I have cut them into triangles, but they could easily be cut into rectangular bars. A few teaspoons of lemon zest would be amazing in here, too.

- 110g/1 stick/4oz butter melted
- 45g/½ cup coconut flour
- 3-5 tbsp granulated sweetener of choice, or more to your taste
- 2 tsp vanilla
- 1 tsp baking powder
- 8 eggs
- 1 cup frozen blueberries

1. Mix together the melted butter, coconut flour, sweetener, vanilla and baking powder until smooth.
2. Add the eggs one by one, mixing in between each one.
3. Pour into a rectangular baking dish, lined with baking parchment.
4. Press each frozen blueberry evenly into the cake. This allows the berries to be evenly distributed and not clump together. It also stops the cake from turning purple!
5. Bake at 180C/350F for 20-25 minutes until cooked in the centre.
6. Once cooled, cut down the centre, then cut across to create the blueberry triangles (or bars).

Blueberry paleo pancakes

Makes	Serving
10 pancakes	1 pancake

Nutrition per serving: Calories: 110 | Total fat: 7.7g | Total carbs: 5.9g | Fibre: 2.2g | Sugars: 2g | Protein: 3.7g

These may just become your go-to pancake recipe. They are virtually foolproof and it's all made in one bowl. Simply mix the wet ingredients, then add the dry ingredients and mix again until smooth. Press your favourite berries into the pancake as it cooks.

- 4 eggs
- 250ml/1 cup coconut cream
- 2 tsp vanilla extract
- 1 tsp baking powder
- 45g/½ cup coconut flour
- 4 tbsp granulated sweetener of choice, or more to your taste
- Salt to taste
- ½ cup blueberries, or berries of choice

1. Mix the eggs, coconut cream and vanilla in a bowl. Whisk until smooth.
2. Add all the dry ingredients (baking powder, coconut flour, sweetener and salt). Mix until the batter is lump-free.
3. Heat some coconut oil in the frying pan. Place a large spoon of the batter into the frying pan and press a few blueberries into each pancake.
4. Cook on a gentle medium heat until golden on the underside, and when the top of the pancake starts to show bubbles coming through. Flip over each pancake to cook on the other side.
5. Optional: serve with whipped coconut cream and more berries. A sprinkling of chopped nuts is a lovely addition, too.

To lower the carb value in the pancakes, simply omit the berries. You may wish to add walnuts or macadamias instead, or add some cinnamon or ginger for extra sweetness.

Chelsea buns

Makes	Serving
6 buns	1 bun

Nutrition per serving: Calories: 246 | Total fat: 18.6g | Total carbs: 13.7g | Fibre: 8.2g | Sugars: 1.6g | Protein: 10g

So light and fluffy, yet stodgy enough to fill up little tummies at lunchtime. Add plenty of cinnamon and sweetener in the centre. Children love unrolling them as they eat each bun.

Low-carb Chelsea bun dough
- 200g/2 cups almond meal/flour
- 40g/½ cup psyllium husk
- 2 tsp baking powder
- 4-8 tbsp granulated sweetener of choice, or more to your taste
- 4 egg whites
- 1 tsp vanilla extract
- 250ml/1 cup boiling water

Cinnamon filling
- 2 tsp ground cinnamon
- 2 tsp granulated sweetener of choice
- Lemon zest (optional)

Glaze
- 4 tbsp powdered sweetener
- 1 tsp vanilla extract (optional)
- Enough water to make a liquid glaze

Low-carb Chelsea bun dough
1. Place all the dry ingredients together in a bowl and mix well.
2. Make a hole in the middle of the dry ingredients and add the egg whites and vanilla. Mix just a little, so you can't see the egg whites anymore.
3. Add a third of the boiling water gently and slowly, mix. Add another third, mix. Add the final third and mix until it looks like a sticky dough.
4. If the dough looks too wet, add an extra tablespoon of psyllium husk. If too dry, add a teaspoon of water at a time.
5. Pour the dough onto a large sheet of baking parchment/paper. Place another piece of baking parchment/paper on top.
6. Press out with your hands until it is a rectangle shape and 1cm/½-inch thick.

Cinnamon filling
1. Mix the cinnamon and sweetener together and sprinkle all over the rolled dough.
2. Using the baking parchment/paper, start to roll the dough up along the longest side.
3. Continue to roll it into one long roll, then cut into even slices.

4. Place each slice in a ring tin that has been oiled and lined.
5. Bake at 180C/350F for 20-30 minutes, or until each Chelsea bun is golden and baked in the centre.

Glaze
1. Mix the powdered sweetener, vanilla and water together to make a liquid glaze.
2. Drizzle, pour or spoon all over.
3. Enjoy warm or cold.

Carrot cupcakes

Makes	Serving
12 cupcakes	1 cupcake with frosting

Nutrition per serving: Calories: 153 | Total fat: 13.8g | Total carbs: 3.9g | Fibre: 1.6g | Sugars: 1.5g | Protein: 3.4g

Everyone loves a classic carrot cake, so if you make little carrot cupcakes and top them with cream-cheese frosting, your kids will love you forever.

Carrot cupcakes
- 5 eggs
- 110g/3.5oz/1 stick butter, melted
- 3 tbsp granulated sweetener of choice, or more to your taste
- 2 tsp vanilla extract
- 150g/5oz/1½ cups carrots, grated/shredded
- 25g/1/4 cup shredded/desiccated coconut, unsweetened
- 22.5g/1/4 cup coconut flour
- 1 tsp ground cinnamon
- 1 tsp mixed spice
- ½ tsp ground nutmeg
- 2 tsp baking powder

Cream-cheese frosting
- 115g/½ cup full-fat cream cheese
- 1-2 tbsp granulated sweetener of choice, or more to your taste

Carrot cupcakes
1. Beat together eggs, melted butter, sweetener and vanilla.
2. Add grated/shredded carrot, coconut, coconut flour, spices and baking powder.
3. Pour into cupcake cases or a lined cupcake tray. Bake at 180C/350F for 10-15 minutes or until a fork comes out clean when pushed in.

Cream-cheese frosting
1. Soften the cream cheese by bringing it to room temperature or placing in the microwave for 10-20 seconds.
2. Stir in 1-2 tbs sweetener of choice.
3. You could also add some lemon zest to give it more flavour.
4. Cover with cream-cheese frosting.

Coconut flour chocolate-chip cookies

Makes	Serving
10 cookies	1 cookie

Nutrition per serving: Calories: 139 | Total fat: 12.3g | Total carbs: 5.1g | Fibre: 3.3g | Sugars: 0.7g | Protein: 2.6g

For those children who attend a school with a nut-free policy, coconut flour chocolate-chip cookies are perfect to pack. Add extra vanilla and sweetener for those new to sugar-free baking. The cocoa nibs add a yummy crunch, and they won't melt in the summer.

- 113g/1 stick butter, softened
- 4 tbsp granulated sweetener of choice, or more to taste
- 65g/⅔ cup coconut flour
- ½ tsp baking powder
- 2 eggs
- 2 tbsp cocoa nibs
- 2 tsp vanilla extract

1. Cream together the softened butter and sweetener until light, pale and fluffy.
2. Add all the other ingredients and mix well until combined and the mixture begins to thicken.
3. Squeeze a small handful into a ball, then press into a cookie shape with your fingers.
4. Place the coconut flour chocolate-chip cookies on a lined baking tray and bake at 180C/350F for 10-15 minutes, or until golden brown on the edges.
5. Allow to cool for a while, then remove and place on a baking rack to cool down completely. These cookies are even nicer the next day.

The slower the changes you make, the better
Build a routine and make it sustainable

DRINKS

Peppermint green smoothie | Flavoured waters

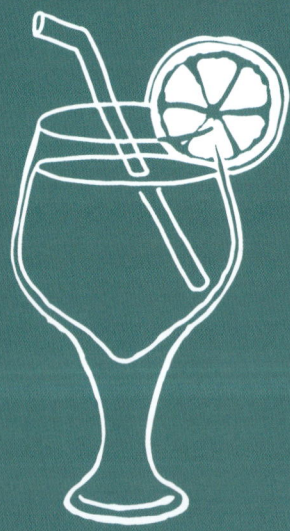

Peppermint green smoothie

Makes	Serving
2 smoothies	1 smoothie

Nutrition per serving: Calories: 241 | Total fat: 18.9g | Total carbs: 13.8g | Fibre: 5.1g | Sugars: 4.8g | Protein: 6g

Most kids automatically turn away from anything green. Want to know the magic trick to make them love green? Turn it into a peppermint smoothie! Don't believe me? Give it a go. This is a low-carb smoothie packed with fibre and protein.

- 1 tbsp chia seeds
- 125ml/½ cup coconut cream
- 125ml/½ cup natural, unsweetened yoghurt
- 250ml/1 cup almond milk (or coconut milk)
- ½ avocado
- A huge handful of leafy greens
- Handful of mint leaves
- Peppermint essence
- Sweetener to taste. How much you will need will vary enormously, so experiment
- 3 ice cubes

1. Place everything in the blender.
2. Turn the blender on and process until no lumps or leaves can be seen.
3. Taste and adjust the sweetness with sweetener.

Flavoured waters

Sending children to school with flavoured waters is a superb way to wean children off fizzy drinks and fruit juice until they are ready for plain water. Flavoured water turns dull tap water into something fun and pretty. Why not make some of these for yourself? We can't let the kids have all the fun!

- Strawberry and lime
- Apple and cinnamon
- Lemon and ginger
- Cucumber and mint
- Lime and mint
- Strawberry and basil
- Ginger and blueberries
- Lime, cucumber and berries
- Raspberry and lime
- Lemon and orange
- Kiwifruit and ginger
- Watermelon and mint

Recipe notes
Transform ice cubes with berries. Just pop two or three berries into each section of an ice-cube tray and fill them with water. As the ice cube melts, the berry is released to eat! Experiment with freezing other fruit, citrus or herbs.

Choose your fruit, herbs and ice cubes then finally add plain or carbonated water.

Remember how far you have come,
not how far you have yet to go

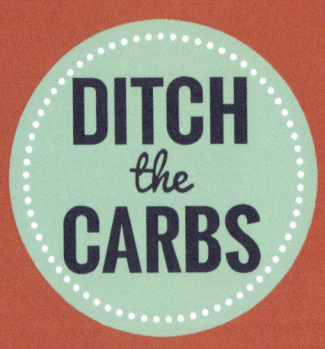

Printed in Poland
by Amazon Fulfillment
Poland Sp. z o.o., Wrocław